Fiddlers Three

A comedy in two acts
(We Don't Want to Lose You and *Cut and Dried*)

Eric Chappell

Samuel French — London
New York - Toronto - Hollywood

Also by Eric Chappell
published by Samuel French Ltd

Double Vision
Haunted
Haywire
Heatstroke (Snakes and Ladders)
It Can Damage Your Health
Natural Causes
Something's Burning
Theft
Up and Coming

WE DON'T WANT TO LOSE YOU

CHARACTERS

Harry, mid-thirties
Rex, mid-thirties
Osborne, mid-twenties
Fletcher, mid-fifties
Norma, early twenties
Ros, Rex's wife, mid-thirties

SYNOPSIS OF SCENES

The action of the play takes place in two adjoining
offices in "Multiple Holdings"

Time — the present

WE DON'T WANT TO LOSE YOU

SCENE 1

The offices of "Multiple Holdings". Late morning

Two offices are seen onstage. A corridor wall runs US *of the offices; the top section of this is made of reeded glass through which passers-by can dimly be seen. The larger office, to the* L, *is the general office; Fletcher's office is to the* R. *The offices are separated by a wood and glass partition with a door in it and a door leads out of the general office* US *into the corridor*

In the general office, facing DS, *are three desks, arranged in order of seniority, so the most senior desk, Rex's, is closest to Fletcher's office, Harry's desk is in the middle and that of Osborne, the most junior, is the furthest away. The desks have in and out trays and other office equipment on them and are piled high with ledgers and tabulations. Tall filing cabinets stand against the walls. There is a coatstand with coats on it for Fletcher, Harry and Rex. Rex's briefcase stands by his desk*

Fletcher's desk is spotlessly tidy, with a desk lamp, phone, papers and a notepad on it. A deep swing chair and a filing cabinet are amongst the room's furnishings

When the CURTAIN *rises Harry, smartly dressed and in his mid-thirties, is sitting with his feet on the middle desk studying the newspaper*

Rex enters from the corridor carrying a pile of tabulations. He is the same age as Harry but looks older. He has a harassed expression and his suit is crumpled. He slams down the tabulations on his already crowded desk and eyes Harry reproachfully

Rex When are you going to start work?

Harry glances towards Fletcher's office

Harry He's not here.
Rex That's not the point. We're here — and contrary to popular rumour we're supposed to start work at nine o'clock — not lunchtime. So get your size tens off that desk and get something done.

Harry straightens up slowly

Harry Don't pull rank on me, Rex.

Rex I'm not pulling rank.

Harry I've known you a long time — just remember that. Don't let success go to your head.

Rex What success?

Harry You may have got Glover's job ...

Rex I haven't got Glover's job. I'm sitting at his desk, that's all.

Harry And remember what happened to him.

Rex I know what happened to him, Harry — and it's going to happen to me if things don't change.

Harry And remember something else — the race isn't always to the swiftest.

Rex Well, that should suit you.

Harry Be nice to people on the way up because you may meet them on the way down.

Rex (*sighing*) I knew it was going to be one of those days. Look, Harry, I've been up half the night with Baby Thing. I don't need this.

Harry Well, don't blame me. It's not my fault you keep potting the black.

Rex I don't keep potting the black! It was planned.

Harry Then why haven't you got a name for it?

Rex We can't think of one.

Harry Don't tell me you've run out of names.

Rex No. We can't decide.

Harry How many is it now — four?

Rex Three.

Harry It must be getting crowded.

Rex Yes. We're thinking of going into the roof.

Harry She should send you into the roof.

Rex Harry, we've got to get on. Fletcher says we have to raise the pace.

Harry turns a page languidly

Harry I can do that.

Rex You? You couldn't raise your eyebrows before eleven-thirty. Do you know where Fletcher is at the moment? With the manager. He's been in there for two hours. The manager wants to know why we haven't balanced.

Harry I should have thought that was obvious. I could see this coming.

Rex I wish you'd told me. I'd have emigrated.

Harry The trouble is we've never been able to replace Glover.

Rex Wait a minute. I replaced Glover.

Harry Precisely. And I replaced you. And Osborne replaced me. But are we getting the rate for the job? No. And that's why Osborne's not pulling his weight. It's made him bitter.

Rex You've made him bitter, Harry. (*He looks around*) Where is he? He's not hanging around Norma's desk again?

Harry No — he's out getting some fresh veg for his mother.
Rex My God! When's he going to learn?

Osborne enters. He is in his mid-twenties with an open, innocent face. He is dressed casually in a corduroy jacket and is carrying a shopping bag. During the following he takes a large cream cake from the bag and tucks into it

Where have you been?
Osborne Getting some Brussels.
Rex Brussels! Why didn't you get some potatoes as well? We could have sat round and peeled them for you.
Osborne What's the matter with you?
Harry He's in a mood.
Rex I'm not in a mood. All I ask, Osborne, is that you take your pen out of your pocket — that's the blue thing next to your comb — and get on with some work.
Osborne You've changed since you got Glover's job.
Harry And you know what happened to him.
Rex I haven't got Glover's job — not yet. (*He pauses*) Anyone heard how he is?
Osborne Still paralysed all down the left side.
Harry Poor bugger. I blame Fletcher. He gave him no support — he showed no confidence in him. Always bringing him those cuttings out of the paper. Jobs abroad. Usually in the frigging Congo, or South America. The further the better. It hardly made him feel wanted.
Rex I don't think that worried old Glover.
Harry Then what did worry him? You were the last person to talk to him. What happened?

Harry and Osborne regard Rex suspiciously

Rex (*realizing the implications of their regard*) Nothing. He was all right when I left him. He was smiling.
Osborne He was smiling when they found him.
Rex The last thing I said to him was that he should slow down.
Harry He's done that all right. He's come to a dead stop.
Rex Look … (*He realizes that Osborne is eating the cake*) What are you doing?
Osborne Eating.
Rex It's almost lunchtime.
Osborne I know. That's why I'm hungry.
Harry Looks disgusting. What is it?
Osborne An elephant's foot.

Rex My God!

Fletcher appears outside the door; he is visible as a shadowy figure through the glass

(*Seeing the shadowy figure*) And 2p …
Harry Check.
Osborne (*swallowing*) Check.

Fletcher enters. He is an elegant, well-groomed man in his mid-fifties with a neat moustache

Rex Good-morning, JF.
Fletcher Is it, Rex? (*He gives Osborne a withering glance*) I've been with the manager all morning. I come back like Moses from the heights bearing his commandments only to find my people feasting and making merry …

Osborne pushes the cake to one side

(*Sharply*) Do you have to have that sign on the back of your van, Osborne?
Osborne What sign, Mr Fletcher?
Fletcher "I'm constipated, I haven't passed a thing all day." Do you think that's funny?
Osborne (*considering*) Yes.
Fletcher Well, unfortunately the manager doesn't share your sense of humour.
Rex (*anxiously*) What commandments, JF?
Fletcher What?
Rex You said you were bearing his commandments.
Fletcher The not unreasonable command that we balance the cash. Is it balanced, Rex?
Rex No.
Fletcher What appears to be the problem?

Rex, Harry and Osborne look at each other

Rex We think it may be a computer virus.
Fletcher (*with a faint smile*) A computer virus. One of the few pleasures of being in this mess is listening to the excuses. I always wonder what you'll come up with next. There's nothing wrong with that computer. Last week I saw it produce the pay roll for the whole company, supervized by a young man in a pink shirt — a young man no older than Osborne. It's a very sophisticated piece of technology.

Osborne The human brain's more complex than the most sophisticated computer.

Fletcher (*acidly*) Is it really? Well, yours may be, Osborne, but the rest of us can only gaze in awe. I know only one certain thing about the computer — if you put rubbish in you'll get rubbish out. And there's plenty of rubbish around here. Now, Rex, what's the position?

Rex The position?

Fletcher How much are we out?

Rex We've rounded it off.

Fletcher Round it off by all means but give it to me straight. I don't want any false optimism. I want the hard facts.

Rex We've brought it down ——

Fletcher Good.

Rex — to a hundred and fifty thousand.

Fletcher (*stunned*) Jesus Christ! (*He slumps into a chair and buries his head in his hands*)

The others regard him anxiously

Osborne (*quietly*) Is he all right?

Rex He said he wanted the hard facts.

Harry I don't think he wanted them that hard.

Fletcher straightens up and takes a deep breath. He stands and flaps his arms loosely by his sides

Fletcher I'm not going to get tense. I shall remain calm. I won't be sacrificed on the altar of commerce. That's what happened to poor Glover. How is he by the way?

Rex Still paralysed all down the left side.

Harry But he is feeding himself.

Fletcher Then we must send him some grapes. Poor Glover, if only he'd learned to slow down.

Osborne We should all learn to relax.

Fletcher (*sharply*) If you relax any more, Osborne, you'll fall out of that bloody chair.

Osborne straightens up hurriedly

(*Leaning over Osborne's desk; menacingly*) I think I should warn you, gentlemen, that storm cones have been hoisted. There's rough weather ahead, and the leaky ships among us may not survive. Do I make myself ... (*He puts his hand on Osborne's cream cake and stops*) My God! (*He regards his hand*) What the bloody hell's this, Osborne?

Osborne An elephant's foot, Mr Fletcher.

Fletcher It's obscene. (*He wipes his hand on his handkerchief*) Rex, this is an office — not a cafeteria. Please remember that. There'll be no more eating in here — not as much as a peppermint — until the cash is balanced.

Fletcher goes into his office and slams the door. He sits at his desk and makes a phone call during the following

Only the conversation in the general office can be heard

Rex (*hissing*) Why do you do this to me, Osborne? Have I said something to offend you — some unkind word, some thoughtless barb? What have you got against me?

Osborne Nothing — you've always been decent to me, Rex.

Rex Then be decent to me and get on with your flaming work.

Osborne No need to shout.

Rex Did I raise my voice? I'm sorry.

Osborne You're lucky to get me on the money they pay here.

Rex (*incredulously*) Who told you that?

Harry I did. Have you seen his pay slip? It's derisory. And he has a widowed mother to support. He should go in there and ask for a rise.

Rex (*hastily*) I wouldn't do that if I were you, Osborne.

Harry Why not? It's sweated labour — right out of Dickens. He could be Bob Cratchit sitting there.

Rex stares at Osborne

Rex Bob Cratchit? Bob Cratchit didn't spend half his day shopping: he was bent over his books, working away in mittens, frightened to put a piece of coal on the fire — that was Bob Cratchit.

Harry I suppose you're sorry those days have gone.

Rex I didn't say that.

Harry Well, if they ever come back we know where to find Scrooge. You should go in there and demand a fair day's pay for a fair day's work, Osborne.

Rex He's not doing a fair day's work.

Harry That's because he's not getting a fair day's pay.

Osborne Right.

Harry And suppose he says no, Osborne?

Osborne Then I'd threaten him with my resignation.

Rex Well, that should send a thrill of fear through him.

Harry Why not? He needs us more than ever now Glover's gone.

Osborne Right.

Rex Will you stop winding him up, Harry? Didn't you hear what Fletcher said? "Storm cones have been hoisted." He may accept Osborne's resignation with tears of gratitude.

Osborne That wouldn't worry me.

Rex Wouldn't it?

Osborne All I need's a push.

Rex And you're going the right way to get one.

Osborne I could always get another job — something more exciting, more interesting. In the open air, the great outdoors, forestry.

Rex Forestry? You don't even like the window open. You won't go out if it's raining.

Harry He can't. His shoes let water. He has to jump over puddles. He can't even afford a decent pair of shoes on the money they pay him.

Rex Don't set him off again.

Osborne rises

Where are you going?

Osborne I thought I'd check these figures with Norma.

Rex Sit down. That's something else I have to tell you. *(He lowers his voice)* Stop trying it on with Norma.

Osborne Why?

Rex Because Fletcher doesn't like it.

Osborne *(grinning)* Fletcher's not going to get it.

Harry chuckles

Rex You're encouraging him again, Harry.

Osborne Don't worry, Rex. I'll be discreet.

Rex You may be discreet but she's not. You always come back with your shirt out.

Harry That's nothing new. At Christmas she pulled everyone's shirt out, and some of them didn't even work here.

Rex I don't care how many shirts she's pulled out. I'm concerned with Osborne at the moment.

Osborne It isn't sexual.

Rex Isn't it?

Osborne Norma says a man can't get fresh, keep his dignity, and tuck his shirt in — all at the same time.

Rex Then you admit you're getting fresh.

Osborne I can't resist her. Not when she's wearing those boots and that skirt.

Rex Well, I'd try, Osborne, for your sake.

Osborne Trouble is, there's someone else — I know there is!

Rex Then accept defeat gracefully, for God's sake.

Fletcher emerges from his office

Harry And 10p.
Rex Check.
Osborne Check.

Fletcher crosses and takes some documents from Osborne's out tray. Something in the tray catches his eye; a paper dart. He picks up the dart and examines it thoughtfully

Osborne looks uneasy

Fletcher raises the dart and flights it across the room. The others watch in silence. Fletcher looks coldly at Osborne

Fletcher Could I have a word, Rex?

Fletcher goes into his office, Rex following

   Osborne takes this opportunity to exit

Harry strains to hear the following conversation

   Close the door, Rex.

Rex closes the door. Fletcher sits in his chair and leans back

Fletcher I see Osborne's been struggling with the problems of flight again.
Rex Yes, JF.
Fletcher Paper darts! What next? Basket weaving? Taj Mahal out of matchsticks? All in the firm's time.
Rex I'll have a word with him.
Fletcher Rex, on the advice of my doctor I've been checking my blood pressure. Well, after poor Glover I thought it advisable.
Rex Indeed.
Fletcher Do you know when I get the highest reading? Not when I've been stuck in traffic and almost crushed by a juggernaut, not when the manager's had me on the mat for two solid hours — no, it's when I come across that little wanker! (*He flaps his hands, trying to relax*) I never thought I'd envy poor Glover. A quiet side ward, tended by gentle nurses, with easy access to an oxygen cylinder — it sounds most attractive.

Rex Perhaps you should be on tranquillizers.

Fletcher I am on tranquillizers! (*He holds up a bottle of tablets*) Something poor Glover left behind. (*He crams a couple of tablets into his mouth*)

Rex With respect, they didn't do him much good, JF. He tried to jump out of the window.

Fletcher Don't remind me. (*He stands and looks into the general office*) My God! Where's Osborne now? The only way to keep him at his desk is to throw a net over the bugger.

Rex He's checking some figures with Norma.

Fletcher That's another thing. I've told you before — he spends far too much time around her desk.

Rex Well, she is an attractive girl, JF.

Fletcher She's what?

Rex Attractive.

Fletcher Is she? I can't say I noticed. But then, thank God, I'm past that sort of thing. I see no beauty in the female form, Rex — I prefer a good sunset these days.

Rex Yes, but Osborne's young — and she does have this cleavage …

Fletcher Oh, yes, I've noticed the cleavage. I've also noticed the crucifix.

Rex Crucifix?

Fletcher She wears it just here … (*He motions to his chest*) Do you know what that means? It means hallowed ground. It means look but don't touch, Rex. Osborne would do well to remember that.

Rex Yes, JF.

Fletcher Although I can't see much point in wearing a crucifix if you're going to dress like a tart. Have a word with her about our dress code, Rex.

Osborne returns to the general office, his shirt tail out at the back. He picks up a ledger and heads for the exit again

Rex and Fletcher observe Osborne's shirt tail

Osborne exits

Did you see that? His bloody shirt's out again, Rex.

Rex I'll have a word with him.

Fletcher No! (*Quietly*) No, it's too late for that, Rex.

Rex What?

Fletcher (*slowly*) The manager wants someone's head on a plate.

Rex I don't understand.

Fletcher Someone has to be responsible for this cock-up.

Rex You mean?

Fletcher I mean we have to give him someone..

Rex Not Osborne.

Fletcher Well, it's not going to be me.

Rex But we can't ——

Fletcher Can't? Would you like me to tell the manager that?

Rex He's got a good brain, JF.

Fletcher Where does he keep it — in a drawer? He has to go — we can't afford to be sentimental. You can't make an omelette without breaking eggs.

Rex But do we have to make an omelette out of Osborne? Couldn't we give him another warning?

Fletcher No, we don't want to put him on his guard. I want to get rid of him before he's out of his probationary period.

Rex Just let me talk to him. It's Harry — he's made Osborne dissatisfied. He feels he's not being paid enough.

Fletcher Not paid enough! Whatever we pay that young shite — it's too much.

Rex Well, I don't envy you, JF, having to tell him.

Fletcher I'm not telling him— you are.

Rex What!

Fletcher He's your responsibility.

Rex But I can't ——

Fletcher Can't! I keep hearing that word. The manager will not tolerate the word can't. This would have been Glover's role had he been here; since you're filling in for him, it's your job.

Rex But I'm only temporary.

Fletcher Yes. How temporary remains to be seen. I'm watching you, Rex. I want to see how you handle this one. I'm looking for maturity — strength of character. If you can't do a little thing like this you'll never make senior management.

Rex Do I have to do it now?

Fletcher The sooner the better.

Rex But he's got a widowed mother. She scrubbed floors to keep him at college.

Fletcher Oh dear. That does pull at the heart strings.

Rex She has a walking frame.

Fletcher Poor soul.

Rex Surely that makes a difference.

Fletcher Yes, you'll have to be extremely gentle with him. I believe there's some red wine left in my filing cabinet. Give him a glass — it'll help to soften the blow. Do it over lunch. (*He produces a small comb and runs it through his moustache*) Now I'm expected in the boardroom …

Rex But, JF, I just don't think I can do it …

Fletcher I'm sure you can. (*He hands Rex the bottle of tablets*) Take a couple of these — they might help. (*He pauses*) Why not give him a couple as well? Then you'll both be relaxed ...

Fletcher exits through the general office

Rex is left staring at the bottle. He returns slowly to his desk

Harry What was all that about?

Rex Osborne. I've got to sack him.

Harry (*shocked*) You can't!

Rex Can't? The manager doesn't like to hear the word "can't", Harry. It's not my decision — it's come from the top.

Harry And you're going to do it — just like that?

Rex No — not just like that. But I've got to do it.

Harry You don't care, do you? You've always been the same. A little power goes straight to your head. All you need is a pair of jackboots and an armband. What have you got against Osborne anyway?

Rex The same thing that you have. Most of the time you can't find him and when you do he's half asleep. He wanders around here like a dormouse in search of hibernation.

Harry That's because he studies all night. He's getting qualified. And you're not qualified, are you? Afraid he might take your job one day?

Rex No! And if this is anyone's fault, it's yours. You made him dissatisfied — you persuaded him that the firm owed him something. You made him bitter.

Harry Bitter! He's going to be bitter all right. And I'll tell you this. Glover wouldn't have done it to him. He had heart. We were a happy team then. They were the good times.

Rex Good times! I don't think Glover would agree with you. He tried to jump out of that window. He had a heart attack, a nervous breakdown, and breathing problems all on the same day. They didn't know which hospital to take him to. And do you know why — because he let it get to him, Harry. He was too sensitive.

Harry Well, no-one can accuse you of that.

Rex You can't make an omelette without breaking eggs.

Harry But Osborne's not an egg. He's your friend.

Rex I know. It's not going to be easy. (*He turns away from Harry, takes a couple of tablets from the bottle and chews them*) And I don't want you telling anyone about this. I don't want him hearing it from someone else.

Harry He won't hear it from me. He's my friend too.

Rex glances at his watch and crosses to Fletcher's office. He takes a bottle of wine and two glasses from Fletcher's cabinet

Norma enters from the corridor. She is attractive and in her early twenties. She is wearing a short skirt, and a cross glitters against her open shirt

Heard the news, Norma? Osborne's getting the bullet.

Rex returns from Fletcher's office looking aghast

During the following, Rex, Harry and Norma cluster round Harry's desk

Norma I know. It's all round the typing pool.
Rex (*stunned*) Is it?
Harry Bad news travels fast.
Norma I can't look him in the face.
Harry Well, someone has to ...
Norma I never realized what large, sad eyes he had. Who could do a thing like that to him?
Harry Have to be someone pretty ruthless, Norma. Be like shooting a cocker spaniel.
Norma His mother has terrible arthritis.
Harry That's from scrubbing all those floors.
Norma She depends on him.
Harry All her hopes dashed ...
Norma What's she going to say when he tells her?
Harry I can see the teacup dropping from those gnarled old hands — hands roughened from years of scrubbing ...
Rex For God's sake! Will you two give it a rest?
Norma What's the matter, Rex?
Harry He's the one who's going to do it.
Norma What!

Osborne enters. He sees them clustered around the desk

Osborne You're all looking very serious. What's the matter?
Rex Nothing. (*He pauses*) Well, when I say nothing ...
Harry (*quickly*) How's your mother, Osborne?
Osborne Not too good. Can hardly cross the room these days — and she's very bent.
Harry All that scrubbing.
Osborne She needs to get away. I'm going to spoil her this year — take her to Spain, stay at a first-class hotel.

Rex (*anxiously*) You haven't booked, have you?

Osborne No. Why?

Rex (*after a hesitation*) You can get some very good bargains if you leave it to the last minute …

Harry (*darkly*) And you never know when the economic climate's going to change …

Norma Ossie, should we go in the park this lunchtime — take our sandwiches?

Osborne (*surprised*) What? You and me?

Norma Why not? We could sit on the river bank — smell the flowers — forget our troubles …

Osborne (*grinning*) What troubles? I haven't got any troubles.

Norma We all have troubles, Ossie. Some we don't even know about … I'll see you in the park.

Norma exits abruptly

Osborne I think this is my lucky day.

Harry I wouldn't be too sure of that.

Osborne What do you mean?

Harry (*hastily*) I mean you're not thinking. It'll be crowded in the park. Get out into the country, somewhere secluded, up in the hills. I always find that your problems seem smaller from up there …

Osborne I haven't got any problems.

Harry Not yet. But who knows — they can come out of a clear blue sky, Osborne.

Osborne Well, I have one problem — my van won't take those hills.

Harry Take my car — I'm not using it. (*He throws his car keys to Osborne*)

Osborne (*staring*) But, Harry — you never let anyone drive your car.

Harry (*fiercely*) I'm letting you drive it, all right?

Harry exits

Osborne That was nice of him.

Rex Yes.

Osborne A date with Norma. I'd better get smartened up. (*He moves to the door*)

Rex Pop back before you go. There's something I want to tell you.

Osborne (*grinning*) I know — another warning. You worry about me like an old hen, Rex. Oh, that reminds me. (*He moves to the shopping bag*) I got this for Baby Thing. I know it's a little late but I didn't know what to get …

Osborne produces an object in a brown paper bag from the shopping bag and gives it to Rex. Rex opens the bag and produces a glove puppet from it

Rex (*staring*) What is it?

Osborne It's a glove puppet. You put it on your hand. See? (*He demonstrates*)

Rex (*staring*) For the baby? (*He looks moved*)

Osborne Yes. What's the matter?

Rex Nothing. But you're the only one who's … No-one else bothered to … I didn't expect …Thanks.

Osborne smiles at Rex's embarrassment

Osborne I'll be back in a minute. (*He moves to the door and pauses*) You know I could never leave this place really — too many friends.

Osborne exits

Rex sighs deeply and pours himself a large glass of wine

Norma enters wearing a coat

Norma Have you told him?

Rex Not yet.

Norma You can't do it, Rex.

Rex Don't blame me, Norma. You're the one who pulled his shirt out.

Norma That was to discourage him.

Rex It didn't work. If he was harassing you — you should have complained.

Norma I've no time for women like that. I can look after myself. Anyway, it would have got him the sack.

Rex He has got the sack.

Norma Then there's nothing I can say to make you change your mind?

Rex No.

Norma Rex, I've always looked up to you. I thought you were different from the rest.

Rex Being different isn't a good idea round here. It doesn't pay to stick your neck out.

Norma turns on her heel and marches towards the exit

Ros, Rex's wife, enters. She is about the same age as her husband and is pretty, plump and equally harassed. She is carrying a carrycot

Norma passes Ros, hardly noticing her, and exits

Ros places the carrycot gingerly on one of the desks

Ros Was that Norma?

Rex Yes.

Ros You didn't say she was attractive.

Rex Didn't I? Ros, I've told you not to bring Baby Thing to the office. Fletcher doesn't like it.

Ros It's lunchtime.

Rex That's not the point.

Ros Do you normally drink wine at lunchtime?

Rex I'm having a bad day.

Ros It's going to get worse.

Rex Why?

Ros I called at the garage …

Rex What did they say about the car?

Ros Don't take it on the motorway.

Rex (*alarmed*) Why not?

Ros Front suspension.

Rex How much?

Ros I've got the estimate. It's expensive … (*She produces the estimate*)

Rex (*shrugging*) You can't put a price on human life, Ros. Let me see. (*He studies the estimate*) My God! It'll have to wait.

Ros What about the price of human life?

Rex We've just reached it. We'll stay off the motorway. I haven't got Glover's job yet — and we can't spend the money before we've got it.

Ros How is he?

Rex Still paralysed down the left side

Ros (*picking up the glove puppet*) What's this?

Rex A glove puppet. Osborne bought it for Baby Thing.

Ros That was nice.

Rex Yes. (*Bitterly*) You put your hand up its back and manipulate it (*he demonstrates*) — and my God, I know how it feels.

Ros What's the matter, Rex?

Rex I've got to sack Osborne.

Ros You can't!

Rex Am I hearing the word "can't"? These things happen. It's not the end of the world.

Ros It will be for him. How would you feel? Remember last year — during the reorganization? When you couldn't find your desk on the office plan and it looked as if you'd been replaced by a rubber plant — and you thought you'd been made redundant? You went to bed with a bottle of whisky.

Rex It doesn't pay to get emotional, Ros.

Ros I feel emotional. Osborne's got a widowed ——

Rex Don't say it. I don't care if she's widowed, crippled, and hanging from a walking frame — I have to do it. You can't make an omelette without breaking eggs.

Ros How would you know? You've never made an omelette. And you can't break an egg, it always runs down your arm.

Rex I have to remain dispassionate.

Ros You can't — you're a very emotional person.

Rex I wouldn't say that.

Ros It's nothing to be ashamed of. When we took the children to see *Bambi* — who was the first to cry?

Rex It wasn't me.

Ros When Bambi lost his mother and it started to snow, I heard you sobbing.

Rex That wasn't me. I'm not emotional. You can't be emotional when you have three children to raise. (*He leans over the carrycot*) You'll learn one day, Baby Thing. This world's not for softies.

Ros (*after a pause*) Rex, did we do wrong having children?

Rex What made you say that?

Ros Do you know how they refer to me on the road? "That woman with three or four kids." I wouldn't mind if they just once said two or three but it's always three or four. You'd think it was a crime.

Rex It's not a crime. We wanted them, Ros — that's all that matters. That's why I have to do this — for their sakes. There's no room in senior management for sentiment.

Ros Well, I've got to pick up the other two … (*She picks up the carrycot*) Don't drink too much. (*She heads for the door*)

Rex No, this is for Osborne. I thought if he had a drink of red wine he wouldn't feel it so much.

Ros (*pausing by the door*) Pity you couldn't have made it hemlock — then he wouldn't feel it at all.

Ros exits

Rex takes a deep drink and solemnly addresses the glove puppet on his hand

Rex Don't look at me like that, old chap. It's not my fault — I'm just the messenger.

Osborne appears in the doorway. He watches Rex

(*Looking up to see Osborne watching him. Covering his confusion*) Have a drink, Osborne.

Osborne I'm driving.

Rex Just one. (*He pours a stiff measure into Osborne's glass*) Bottoms up.

Rex downs his drink in a gulp

Osborne I thought you were supposed to sip it.

Rex It's not vintage, Osborne. (*He pauses*) We haven't known each other very long, have we?
Osborne No.
Rex No, but in that time I think we've become friends ... That's why I feel I can tell you this — although it's not easy ... (*He takes another deep drink*)

Osborne watches Rex

Something happened today. I'm afraid it's bad news. (*Hastily*) But not too bad. I mean it's not life or death or anything. After all, it's a big world out there — full of opportunity. Who needs this place? Who needs security? Security can be stifling. (*He sighs*) I only wish I were younger, that's my regret. (*Pause*) Do you know what I'm trying to say, Osborne?
Osborne Yes. And I'm glad you feel you could tell me.
Rex Are you?
Osborne I could see it coming.
Rex You could?
Osborne Yes. (*He gives a bitter glance towards Fletcher's office*) The bastard.
Rex (*sympathetically*) Yes.
Osborne So he's finally sacked you.
Rex What!
Osborne I can't say I'm surprised. The writing's been on the wall for sometime.
Rex Has it?

Osborne replenishes Rex's glass

Osborne Well, I'm not going to let them do this to you, Rex. Not without a fight. They can't manage without the two of us.
Rex What?
Osborne When I come back after lunch I'm going to go straight in there and resign. If you go — I go.
Rex (*faltering*) But, Osborne ——
Osborne I couldn't just stand by and let it happen, Rex, not to you.

Rex gives Osborne a wild stare and turns away. He blows his nose vigorously

Are you all right, Rex?

Rex gives a muffled sob

The Lights fade

CURTAIN

The offices of "Multiple Holdings". Early afternoon

The CURTAIN *rises. Rex, Harry and Osborne are working at their desks. Norma is by the cabinets, doing some filing*

Fletcher enters from the corridor and crosses to his office

Fletcher Would you come through, Rex.

Rex follows Fletcher into the office and closes the door. Only their conversation can be heard during the following

Well, how did he take it?
Rex I didn't tell him.
Fletcher What!
Rex I couldn't. As we were talking I noticed that his cuffs were frayed and his collar was a little dingy — and he'd got these big, sad eyes. He reminded me of Bambi.
Fletcher Bambi! I don't care if he reminded you of Dumbo the elephant — it has to be done. Now I suppose I'll have to do it. And I don't want to hear any more about his frayed cuffs, or his widowed mother and her climbing frame. (*He holds out his hand*)

Rex hands Fletcher the tranquillizers

I'm not a monster, Rex. Do you think I wanted this life. All I ever wanted was a few lobster pots off the Dorset coast — feel the sea breeze ruffling my hair, the firm pull of the oars, the salty spray of an early morning ... (*He gulps down tablets*) Send him in, Rex.

Rex returns to the general office

Rex Osborne, Mr Fletcher wants to see you.
Osborne (*winking*) And I want to see him.

Osborne goes into Fletcher's office, closes the door and sits

Only the conversation in the general office can be heard during the following

Harry (*whispering*) Is this it then?

Rex mimes tapping and breaking an egg

Rex Omelette time, Harry
Harry Poor old Osborne.
Norma How can JF do it to him?
Rex He's on tranquillizers.
Norma (*slamming a drawer*) And what are you on, Rex?
Rex What do you mean?
Norma Why don't you do something — instead of just standing by?
Rex What can I do? It's every man for himself, Norma.
Harry He should have kept his head down.
Norma He'd have stood up for you.
Harry He's an idealist.
Norma He also has a widowed mother.
Rex Don't mention her gnarled old hands, please, not at the moment.
Norma I suppose that makes you feel uncomfortable. I'm disappointed in
   you, Rex — I expected better … (*She moves to the door*)
Harry Wait a minute. Aren't you disappointed in me?
Norma No.

Norma exits

Osborne returns from Fletcher's office looking serious

Rex and Harry watch Osborne furtively

*Osborne sits at his desk and begins to remove objects from his drawer. He
stares at the objects for a moment and then looks up*

Osborne He's sacked me.
Harry Bad luck, Ossie.
Rex Don't worry — it could be a good thing.
Harry You said all you needed was a push.
Osborne Well, I've certainly had that. (*Pause*) You knew, didn't you?
Rex We sort of guessed.
Osborne And you didn't do anything?
Rex You'll soon get fixed up.
Harry A bright boy like you.
Rex I only wish I were younger.
Harry I mean, who wants to work here?
Osborne Well, obviously you two do. You're clinging like limpets. They've
   really sucked the life out of you, haven't they? To think I could be like you
   in twenty years' time. Twitching with fear, terrified of losing my job. Well,
   I haven't lost my spirit, not yet. I —— (*He stops abruptly*)
Rex What's the matter?

Osborne I think I'm going to be sick.

Osborne exits rapidly

Rex and Harry stare at each other

Harry I just hope you're satisfied.
Rex What!

Ros enters

Ros Osborne's being sick in the corridor.

Rex looks anxiously towards Fletcher's office and guides Ros behind the cabinets

Rex Ros, I've told you not to come here.
Ros I was passing.
Rex Passing's fine — just keep going.
Ros I thought I ought to tell you about the chimney-pot.
Rex What chimney-pot?
Ros The one I said was rocking in the wind and you said was as steady as a rock.
Rex What about it?
Ros It's dropped off.
Rex Dropped off! It didn't hit anyone?
Ros No.

Rex gives a sigh of relief

Fortunately they weren't in the car.
Rex What car?
Ros Next door's car — it went through the roof.
Rex What did they say?
Ros They'll send us an estimate.
Rex Are we insured?
Ros I couldn't find chimney-pots in the policy.
Rex It'll cost a fortune.

Harry joins them at the cabinets

Harry At least you've got a job.
Ros Osborne?

Both Rex and Harry mime breaking an egg

Ros So that's why he was sick. Well, I hope you're satisfied, Rex.
Rex Don't you start.

*Norma enters and puts some letters in Rex's tray. She pauses, then shakes
her head sadly at Rex*

Norma Osborne's fainted.

Norma exits

Rex What does she expect me to do? Threaten to resign?
Harry That's an idea. We'll threaten to resign. All for one and one for all.
Shoulder to shoulder. We could bring him to his knees.
Rex Are you sure?
Harry They can manage without Osborne — but not the three of us — they'll
never get the figures out.
Rex That's true.
Ros They can't do without you, Rex.
Rex No-one's indispensable, Ros.
Ros You are.
Rex Who told you that?
Ros You did.
Harry You're worth three of Fletcher, Rex..
Rex I wouldn't say three exactly …
Harry You are, and he knows it. Go in there and tell him. We're not putting
up with this.
Rex (*after a hesitation*) What about you?
Harry You're senior. I'll go in after you. We'll pile on the pressure. He'll
go down like a pricked balloon.
Rex (*doubtfully*) What do you think, Ros?
Ros I don't know what to say. (*She holds up the glove puppet*) All I know
is he bought this for Baby Thing with his last pay cheque ...
Rex I'll have a word with him. You'd better go.

Ros heads for the door and hesitates by it

Ros Just threaten to resign, Rex.
Rex Right.

Ros exits

Rex goes into Fletcher's office. Fletcher swings round in his chair

Fletcher Yes, Rex?
Rex It's about Osborne.
Fletcher He's dismissed.
Rex I know. I think you should reconsider.
Fletcher Why?
Rex Because he's being made a scapegoat.
Fletcher Correct. Was there anything else?
Rex Yes. If Osborne does go — I shall have to seriously consider my position
    here …
Fletcher What does that mean?
Rex It could mean my resignation.
Fletcher Are you resigning?
Rex (*after a hesitation*) I'm threatening to resign.
Fletcher If he goes?
Rex Yes.
Fletcher Then you are resigning?
Rex (*after a pause*) Only if he goes.
Fletcher He's going. And I accept your resignation. Better put it in writing
    — I'd like it this afternoon. I'll need to find a replacement. There's always
    Harry, I suppose …
Rex He's resigning too.
Fletcher Is he resigning or merely threatening to resign?
Rex Both.
Fletcher We'll see should we? Now if there's nothing else — I have some
    phone calls to make … (*He hands Rex the tranquillizers*)

Rex returns to the main office in a daze. He sits at his desk

Harry I bet that gave him something to think about.
Rex Not for long.
Harry What do you mean?
Rex He accepted my resignation. He was almost grateful. You said he'd go
    down like a pricked balloon.
Harry He's bluffing.
Rex Well, we'll soon find out. Better go in there and pile on the pressure.
Harry Pile on the pressure?
Rex Go in there and resign.
Harry Wait a minute. Let's think about this.
Rex What's there to think about?
Harry It's obviously not working. What purpose would it serve?
Rex It would make me feel a hell of a lot better.

Harry Don't worry, I'll do it — tomorrow.
Rex Tomorrow!
Harry He's on those tranquillizers — they're giving him false courage.
Rex Perhaps you should take some. (*He offers Harry the bottle*)
Harry Tomorrow they'll have worn off — that'll be the time. Don't worry, your resignation is just the beginning. This is a war of nerves.

Norma enters

Norma, you won't believe this. Fletcher's accepted Rex's resignation.

Norma sits down by Rex's desk and looks concerned

Norma Oh, Rex — I feel dreadful.
Rex Funny — so do I.
Norma That took some courage.
Harry It certainly did — especially with four kids.
Rex Three, Harry.
Norma (*taking Rex's hand*) It couldn't have been easy — I'm proud of you, Rex.
Harry (*jealously*) I'm doing it tomorrow.
Norma Do you know what I'm going to do?
Rex (*hopefully*) Resign?
Norma I'm going to establish a smile-free zone in the vicinity of the office.
Rex What's that?
Norma No-one smiles around here until Fletcher climbs down.
Rex I don't think I'll find that difficult. I may never smile again. But do you think he'll notice?
Norma He'll notice. He's going to see exactly how we feel.
Harry Norma's right. We won't even speak to him, except in the line of business. And we're all on a go-slow until Rex and Osborne are reinstated.
Rex I don't know about a go-slow, Harry. Around here, that could actually speed things up.

Fletcher opens his office door. He observes the straight faces of his staff then passes through the office with a broad smile

Fletcher exits

Pity we didn't tell him about the smile-free zone. He's smiling enough for all of us.
Harry It won't last. (*He holds up the bottle of tablets*) We've got the tranquillizers.

Norma (*taking the bottle*) They're not tranquillizers. Mr Glover took those for constipation.

Norma exits

Rex Well, they're certainly working for me!

Harry So what we've got here is the placebo effect.

Rex You're not waiting for that to wear off as well, are you? Go after him — resign. Pile on the pressure. You'll probably find him in the Gents.

Harry Wait a minute. I'll have to discuss it with Grace first.

Rex What?

Harry After all, you discussed it with Ros.

Rex Well, yes but ——

Harry It's only fair.

Rex You didn't say anything about discussing it with Grace.

Harry We're man and wife, Rex. What affects me affects her. (*Pause*) Trouble is I know what she's going to say ...

Rex What is she going to say, Harry?

Harry Well, one of her principles in life is: never resign — stay and fight. That's what she'll say.

Rex But this was your idea.

Harry No, I said threaten to resign. You obviously gave yourself no room to manoeuvre.

Rex Well, you certainly have.

Harry Always give yourself room to manoeuvre.

Rex Is that another of Grace's principles?

Harry It is, as a matter of fact.

Rex It's a bloody pity I didn't know about Grace's principles before I went in there.

Osborne enters looking concerned

Osborne Rex, I've just heard you've resigned.

Rex Yes but that's not the latest news. Do you know the latest news, Osborne? We've been let down. Mr All-for-one-and-one-for-all has turned out to be Mr-all-for-himself. Harry's not going to resign.

Harry I didn't say that.

Rex He's going to stay and fight. I'm not sure what he's going to stay and fight for but I've got a damned good idea. (*He puts a hand on Osborne's shoulder*)Well, at least we have our integrity, Ossie. We've kept our self-respect. We'll leave here with our heads held high. We'll go out of that door together.

Osborne (*quietly*) We won't, Rex.

Rex What?

Osborne I'm not leaving.

Rex Not leaving?

Osborne I've been reinstated.

Rex (*staring*) Reinstated! How?

Osborne I went to see the manager ... I pleaded with him. I told him about my mother. I begged. I asked him to give me another chance. Then there was this phone call from JF. That put him in a good mood and he said I could stay as we might be short-staffed.

Rex But where does this leave me, Osborne?

Osborne I'm not sure.

Harry I'll tell you where this leaves you. You said you'd resign unless Osborne was reinstated. He's been reinstated, so there's no need to resign. See Fletcher when he comes back and withdraw your resignation.

Rex And suppose he won't let me?

Osborne Then I'll go in there and threaten to resign unless you're reinstated.

Rex Don't start that again!

Harry If he won't reinstate you — threaten to sue him for constructive dismissal.

Rex studies Harry suspiciously for a moment

Rex You seem to have thought of everything, Harry.

Fletcher enters from the corridor. He moves into his office, humming cheerfully

Harry Now, while he's in a good mood.

Rex I think I know why he's in a good mood. Just watch it change. (*He knocks on the door of Fletcher's office, enters and closes the door*)

Fletcher (*looking up*) Yes, Rex.

Rex Regarding my resignation.

Fletcher A wise move, Rex. I only wish I were younger. And it's not as if you were making any progress here.

Rex Wasn't I?

Fletcher The manager agreed with me.

Rex Did he? And does he wish he were younger too?

Fletcher Do I detect a note of sarcasm, Rex?

Rex Mr Fletcher, my resignation was a protest against Osborne's dismissal.

Fletcher Was it?

Rex Yes. Now he's been reinstated I wish to withdraw it.

Fletcher Ah, but unfortunately wheels have been set in motion. The manager has informed the Chairman.

Rex The Chairman!

Fletcher You should get a personal letter from him this afternoon thanking you for your years of service. Well, when I say a personal letter — it would be a facsimile of his own hand ... But he'll most certainly sign it.

Rex They haven't wasted much time.

Fletcher They wanted someone's head, Rex ... and you put yours on the block. Now, what are your plans?

Rex I haven't got any.

Fletcher Haven't got any! Are you sure? Come, Rex, no-one takes a step like this without making plans — it would be foolhardy. You've been head-hunted, haven't you?

Rex No. I haven't got anywhere to go.

Fletcher Really. Well, that does make your resignation seem rather hasty.

Rex Not as hasty as the personal letter from the Chairman in a facsimile of his own hand!

Fletcher Never mind. A man of your ability will soon find something. Have you thought of franchises?

Rex Franchises.

Fletcher They seem to be the thing. Pronto-print — engraving on glass — take-away spuds. The field appears to be limitless.

Rex I just don't know what I'm going to tell Ros.

Fletcher Doesn't she know?

Rex No.

Fletcher I think you should have kept her fully informed, Rex. After all, it's a big step. And with three or four children ——

Rex Two or three.

Fletcher Two or three?

Rex Three.

Fletcher You don't seem very sure. But then you don't seem very sure of anything. You really should have given this more thought. (*He sighs*) I suppose I'll have to do something ... (*He fidgets among his papers*)

Rex Would you, JF?

Fletcher I can't let you go without showing some concern for your future ... (*He passes Rex a newspaper cutting*) I saw this in today's *Telegraph*. Thought of you instantly. A wonderful opportunity. Tremendous prospects. High salary. Good allowances.

Fletcher guides Rex out of the door

You should seriously consider it. You could live on your expenses and come home a rich man ...

Rex Come home? Where from?

Fletcher Zambia. (*He closes his door*)

Rex is left staring at the cutting

The Lights fade

CURTAIN

SCENE 3

The offices of "Multiple Holdings". Evening

When the CURTAIN *rises the overhead Lights in the main office are on; Fletcher's desk light burns too*

Harry is sitting at Rex's desk, working

Rex enters

Rex (*sharply*) What are you doing at my desk?
Harry What?
Rex You're sitting in my chair.
Harry I was looking for cash receipts.
Rex Well, do it in your own chair.

Harry moves slowly back to his desk

Harry I would point out that it's Glover's chair.
Rex What?
Harry Now I'm sitting in your chair.
Rex Temporarily, this is my chair.
Harry Yes, temporarily's the word. Fletcher wants me to start a collection.
Rex He doesn't waste much time, does he?
Harry I didn't want the job.
Rex I don't suppose you turned it down.
Harry I couldn't very well do that. Someone has to do it. I'm not looking forward to it, Rex.
Rex I suppose not.
Harry It's not as if you're popular.
Rex What?
Harry So I thought if I started the list with twenty pounds, it might shame the others.
Rex (*impressed*) You'd put in twenty pounds?
Harry Not at the moment — I'm short. But they won't know that. Should get a decent present out of it — and something for Ros, possibly a bouquet.
Rex Better make it smelling salts.

Harry You haven't told her yet?

Rex No.

Harry I wouldn't leave it too long.

Rex I don't know how to. I've always told her I was important to the company. I thought I was important.

Harry (*sighing*) It's been a lesson to me.

Rex Has it? (*Suspiciously*) What are you doing here? You never work overtime.

Harry I thought I'd better get to grips with everything. Appraise myself of the problems. After all, there's only Osborne — it's all going to fall on my shoulders.

Rex You don't think they're going to put you in charge?

Harry Why not?

Rex They'll bring someone in.

Harry I don't think so.

Rex (*frowning*) Have you been talking to Fletcher?

Harry Only in the line of business.

Rex Well, as long as you didn't smile.

Harry He didn't get a smile out of me.

Rex I bet he was smiling.

Harry Why?

Rex Because it's laughable. You had six weeks holiday last year. The Chairman only gets four.

Harry I was off sick.

Rex Off sick! You rang me from Heathrow. I couldn't hear you above the roar of jet engines. And you're a bad time-keeper. You arrive late and leave early.

Harry It's not when you get here, or when you leave. It's what you do while you're here.

Rex What's that supposed to mean?

Harry We still haven't balanced the cash. There's still the little matter of a hundred and fifty thousand ...

Rex You bugger! I bet you've got it hidden somewhere.

Harry What are you talking about?

Rex The light's beginning to dawn. It was you who set Osborne up — it was you who set me up. You know where that hundred and fifty thousand is, don't you? You've got it tucked away somewhere.

Harry Rex, I'm not going to take this personally. You're distressed. You've had a bad day. You should talk this over with Ros. A trouble shared is a trouble halved.

Rex Not in our house — a trouble shared is a trouble doubled.

Harry I think you'll be surprised how well she takes it. Probably get a job. Counter work. In the evenings. McDonalds.

Rex McDonalds. My wife shovelling chips. Fuck off!
Harry I'm going to forget you said that, Rex. (*He puts on his coat*) I'm going to leave before we quarrel.
Rex I've got news for you — we have quarrelled.

Harry heads for the door. As he reaches it:

Ros enters with some shopping

Ros Hallo, Harry.
Harry (*sadly*) Ros.
Ros How's Grace? I haven't seen her for ages.
Harry She was saying the same thing. Why don't you come round for dinner sometime?
Ros We'd love to, Harry — but it's not easy to get a sitter.
Harry Bring the kids.
Ros (*surprised*) Bring them?
Harry Yes. We haven't seen them for ages. They must have grown. You know how Grace loves children. She envies you. (*He sighs*) If only nature had smiled at her ... 'Night.

Harry exits

Ros That was nice.
Rex (*coldly*) Was it?
Ros They haven't asked us round since they had that cream carpet fitted. Sad, really — that nature's never smiled on Grace.
Rex It can't, she's on the pill.
Ros That wasn't very kind.
Rex I don't feel very kind. I can't stand his hypocrisy. (*He frowns*) Where are the children?
Ros Mother's. I took them there after Casualty. Then I seized on the opportunity for some late-night shopping. I thought you could help me home with it ...
Rex Wait a minute. You said Casualty.
Ros Jamie's swallowed a steel ball.
Rex Are you sure?
Ros Well, I couldn't find it anywhere. Mind you, they couldn't find it on the X-ray either. I suppose it could have slipped down the settee.
Rex What did they say?
Ros We have to study his motions.
Rex What?
Ros See if he passes it.

Rex My God. Who'd have kids.

*Norma enters. She goes into Fletcher's office and picks up some papers.
She returns through the office, smiling at Rex and Ros*

Ros watches Norma intently

Norma exits

Ros I suppose you feel trapped. I suppose you feel marriage is a handicap.
Rex Of course it's a handicap. Do you think I'd feel as worried as this if I
 wasn't married?
Ros And what about my handicap? Three children, two bags of shopping and
 a pram with a wobbly wheel. Young mothers drive by me in the rain,
 talking into their mobiles, while I plod along in the puddles. And to think
 that at school I told them I wanted to be a ballerina.
Rex (*staring*) A ballerina! You?
Ros That's what I told the class — when we had to say what we wanted to
 be when we grew up. Now they see me and say; "Remember her, she
 wanted to be a ballerina, look at her now."

Norma enters. She crosses to the filing cabinets and takes out some papers

Ros watches her

Norma exits

Does Norma usually work late?
Rex Sometimes.
Ros So you're not always on your own..
Rex No.
Ros (*after a pause*) Why do you work so much overtime, Rex?
Rex Because we're busy and because they pay me a small allowance, a
 pittance for doing it. And we need the money. Late night shopping.
 Couldn't you get enough shopping done in the day? When you enter Asda
 the tills start ringing. (*He looks at Ros's shopping*) Look at this bumper box
 of baby food. She'll be eating this until she's a teenager.
Ros I got the bumper box so that I can enter her for a beautiful baby
 competition.
Rex (*staring*) Baby Thing?
Ros Yes. Why not?
Rex Because she'll never win a beautiful baby competition — one ear's
 lower than the other.
Ros How do you know?

Rex I measured them.

Ros You measured our baby's ears?

Rex It's a pity you didn't. Then you wouldn't have gone in for this needless extravagance. You object to me working overtime. I could be in Zambia.

Ros Zambia!

Rex You wouldn't see me then. I'd get leave every three years — and probably die of dysentery. There are snakes the size of garden hoses; there are hook worms that come up through your boot, up your leg, and into your intestines — you never get rid of them. And you go out and get a bumper box of baby food. (*He buries his head in his hands*)

Ros Oh. My God! (*She sits*) They've accepted your resignation.

Rex Yes. They reinstated Osborne and sacked me.

Ros Why can't they reinstate you?

Rex Osborne crawled — I can't do that.

Ros (*putting her hand on his arm*) I don't want you to crawl. You'll get another job.

Rex Will I? I rang the Jobcentre. All they had to offer was something in sewerage. I'd stink to high heaven and you'd have to wash my overalls. Mind you, I'll soon adapt. I've been up to my neck in shit for years!

Ros You're not going into sewerage. I'll get a job.

Rex What about Baby Thing? Deprived of a mother's love — left with some gin-sodden babyminder.

Ros I was thinking of you.

Rex So was I. Ros, I will be gin-sodden if I don't get a job.

Ros You'll get a job. (*She pauses. Thoughtfully*) Rex, you did resign over Osborne? You're not leaving for any other reason?

Rex No, it's all because of Osborne. Why do you ask?

Ros I just wondered. I'll see you when you get home. You're obviously busy. (*She moves to the door*)

Osborne enters and moves to take his coat from the stand

Osborne (*brightly*) Hallo Ros.

Ros Drop dead.

Ros exits

Osborne I suppose she's mad at me.

Rex You could say that.

Osborne It's not my fault. I didn't ask you to stick your neck out, Rex.

Rex No, I suppose not.

Osborne You've got to keep your head down — look after number one. No-one's indispensable. I realized that in the Gents just now. I was swirling the water around the washbasin when it came to me.

Rex What did?

Osborne Well, there was I making a big splash and then I stopped — within a few seconds it was as still as a mill pond. That's office life — we think we're making a big splash but afterwards it's as if we've never been here — once we've gone there's not even a ripple — that's how much we're missed. That's how much you'll be missed, Rex.

Rex (*leaping up*) You ungrateful little toad. I'd like to strangle you, Osborne.

Osborne backs away

Osborne I know you feel bitter, Rex, but I didn't ask you to resign, did I? You can't blame me.

Rex (*after a pause*) No, I suppose not.

Norma enters

Osborne gives her the smile of the favourite

Osborne Norma, I'm thinking of going clubbing. Would you like to come?

Norma regards Osborne coldly

Norma Shove off, Osborne.

Osborne Oh. (*Crestfallen*) Good-night, then.

No-one answers

Osborne exits

Norma Little shit.

Rex There's no point in blaming Osborne — it's not his fault.

Norma (*sitting by Rex's desk*) No — it's mine. I should have kept quiet.

Rex It has nothing to do with you, Norma. If anyone created this situation, it was Harry.

Norma Harry?

Rex I think he planned the whole thing.

Norma No. It wasn't Harry who accepted your resignation. He's just seizing the opportunity.

Rex Perhaps you're right. I certainly made it easy for him.

Norma You did it because of me — I feel terrible.

Rex Will you stop blaming yourself? (*He takes Norma's hand*) I stuck my neck out. Osborne's right, I shouldn't have done that.

Norma (*looking down at Rex's hand*) Why are you staying? You don't owe them anything.

Rex I thought I'd start to clear my desk.
Norma Clear it. I'm surprised you don't want to burn it. Let's go for a drink.
Rex I should be getting home.
Norma Well, it was just a thought.

Rex studies Norma

Rex Osborne says that when I go from here, I won't leave a ripple. Do you think that's true?
Norma No. You'll leave a ripple.
Rex Harry says I'm unpopular.
Norma Not with me.
Rex (*looking surprised*) I didn't realize.
Norma Other people have.
Rex What other people?
Norma Why do you think Fletcher accepted your resignation?
Rex Why?
Norma He was jealous.
Rex You mean — you and Fletcher? I don't believe it! Osborne said there was someone else.
Norma (*softly*) No — that someone else wasn't Fletcher — it was you …

Rex slowly removes his hand

Rex Norma, I've just lost my job. I've a family to support. I've enough problems already.
Norma Perhaps I shouldn't have said anything. (*She rises*) But since you were leaving …
Rex (*after a hesitation*) What makes you think he's jealous? He told me he wasn't interested in the female form — he prefers a good sunset these days.
Norma Does he? Well, he's not admiring the sunset when he's standing at the bottom of the stairs, pretending to read the notice-board and rattling his change.
Rex (*staring*) Pretending to read the notice-board and rattling his change. Why should he do that?
Norma He's waiting.
Rex Waiting? What for?
Norma For me to come down the stairs — so that he can look up my skirt.
Rex No. Not JF. He's complained about your skirts. That sort of thing doesn't interest him. All he wants these days is a few lobster pots off the Dorset coast. Feel the spray and tang of the sea breeze.
Norma Then why is he staying tonight? (*She nods to Fletcher's coat on the coat stand*) He never works overtime.
Rex Why?
Norma Because I'm here.

Rex Oh.

Norma The only reason I am safe is because you're here.

Rex (*slowly*) I see … So … If I were to go — you wouldn't be safe?

Norma No.

Rex There could be an incident.

Norma Possibly …

Rex And if I were to come back — unexpectedly — say for my briefcase …

Norma Who knows what you'd find …

Rex It's getting late … (*He picks up his briefcase and places it carefully on the other side of the desk*)

Norma I didn't realize you were so devious, Rex.

Rex I'm learning, Norma.

Norma It would be blackmail …

Rex (*smiling*) That's right.

Norma (*after a hesitation*) Why should I?

Rex (*moving closer*) Because then I'll buy you that drink.

Fletcher enters from the corridor and stands by the door watching Norma and Rex

Norma and Rex realize they are being watched and move apart. Norma goes into Fletcher's office and sets to work at the filing cabinet

Fletcher Still here, Rex? I must say I'm surprised, under the circumstances. I think you should get home, have a talk with Ros — you have a lot to tell her.

Rex That's true.

Fletcher Fresh fields and pastures new, Rex. Scan the "Situations Vacant". God! I wish I were your age. And if you need a reference — you know where to come. And I can assure you it'll be glowing.

Rex Thanks, JF. (*He glances into Fletcher's office, where Norma is working*) I'll get off, then … (*He moves to the door and picks up his coat*)

Fletcher Oh, Rex — you've forgotten your briefcase.

Rex picks up the case and exits

Fletcher stands regarding Norma through the open door of the office. He rattles the change in his pocket through the following

Will you be long, Norma?

Norma Just finishing off.

Fletcher Did Rex mention my concern over our dress code?

Norma Yes.

Fletcher It's not that I object personally, you have nice legs — but it may be an incitement to people with less self-control … (*He rattles his change more loudly*)

Norma I'll bear that in mind.

Fletcher I see them hanging about your desk sometimes, like a wolf pack that hasn't killed for a month — almost slavering. If you feel threatened — you will come to me?

Norma Of course. Who else would I come to? (*She takes the bottle of wine and two glasses from the filing cabinet*) Should we have a drink on it? (*She pours two glasses of wine*)

Fletcher Why not? (*He looks cautiously around the general office and sighs*) They will leave all the lights on. (*He crosses and switches off the main lights so that only his desk light is burning. He joins Norma at the desk and takes a glass of wine*)

They sip their drinks

May I ask you something. Norma? The crucifix. Does it have religious significance?

Norma It's not a crucifix. It's an iron cross.

Fletcher An iron cross?

Norma It's quite heavy. Feel. (*She leans forward*)

Fletcher takes the cross gingerly in his hand

Fletcher You're right. It is heavy. An iron cross ... (*He continues to hold the cross*) Weren't they awarded for gallantry in the field?

Norma I believe so.

Fletcher Oh. Did you tremble?

Norma Did I?

Fletcher (*releasing the cross*) I hope my hand wasn't too cold.

Norma No — it was surprisingly warm.

Fletcher My circulation has improved since I got the sunbed ...

Norma I thought you were brown.

Fletcher Yes. (*Confidently*) I'm this colour all over.

Norma Oh. May I see?

Fletcher shyly unbuttons his shirt

(*Peering in*) Oh yes. You are brown.

They are very close. Norma slips her hand inside Fletcher's shirt. Fletcher flicks off the light. There are the sounds of scuffling and the scraping of furniture in the darkness; Norma and Fletcher move behind the desk and on to the floor. Fletcher's shirt-tail gets pulled out

Rex enters the main office from the corridor and switches on the lights

Norma and Fletcher rise up from behind the desk. Fletcher looks flustered. Norma calmly picks up a notepad

Norma Was there anything else, Mr Fletcher?
Fletcher What?
Norma Anything else you'd like me to take down...?
Fletcher Er, no — that will be all, Norma.

Norma crosses by Rex and gives him a broad smile. She exits

Rex regards Fletcher. Fletcher looks flustered

Glad you came along, Rex.
Rex (*coldly*) Are you?
Fletcher I suddenly realized. How it would look. Alone here with an attractive female employee. I could have been compromised. One has to be so careful these days.
Rex Is that why you switched off the lights?
Fletcher We were just leaving. But that's my point. How suspicious that would look to people — to you, even.
Rex Yes.
Fletcher Although the idea's laughable really. A man in my state of health. Hardly the strength to rake up a few leaves these days. Don't be fooled by this tan, Rex — underneath there's a ghastly pallor. Now, I must go, or Mrs Fletcher will be presenting me with a burnt offering. (*He moves towards the exit, revealing for the first time that his shirt-tail is out*)
Rex Mr Fletcher, your shirt's out.
Fletcher What?
Rex At the back.
Fletcher (*hurriedly tucking his shirt in*) So it is.
Rex And there's lipstick on your collar.
Fletcher Is there? (*He becomes busy with his handkerchief*) That's the trouble with these tiny offices: such confined spaces, everyone on top of each other. The sooner they bring in the open-plan the better. Thank you for telling me, Rex. What would Mrs Fletcher have thought?
Rex Yes. How is she these days?
Fletcher Mrs Fletcher? Still can't stand the strong light — and the leg's no better but apart from that ...
Rex I must make a point of seeing her.
Fletcher (*anxiously*) Why?
Rex To say goodbye. After all, I'm leaving.

They look at each other for a long moment

Fletcher (*slowly*) Leaving. Who said you were leaving?

Rex You did. You accepted my resignation.

Fletcher That was in the heat of the moment, Rex. But on reflection, I ask myself, where would I find another like you? A colleague as loyal and trustworthy. Certainly not around here. I may be old-fashioned but those qualities matter more to me than intelligence. Loyalty, trust — discretion. And I'll tell the manager that. I'll go to him in the morning and tell him you wish to withdraw your resignation.

Rex Suppose he won't let me?

Fletcher Then I'll threaten to resign.

Rex (*sighing*) JF — that's how all this started! No-one's indispensable.

Fletcher I am, Rex — the manager's my brother-in-law. Good-night.

Fletcher exits

Rex stands for a moment and then punches the air in victory

The Lights fade

CURTAIN

FURNITURE AND PROPERTY LIST

SCENE 1

On stage: GENERAL OFFICE
Tall filing cabinets containing files
Three desks. *On them*: in and out trays, ledgers, tabulations, office equipment etc.
    By **Rex**'s *desk*: Rex's briefcase
    On **Harry**'s *desk*: newspaper
    On **Osborne**'s *desk*: paper dart in out tray
Chairs
Coatstand. *On it*: coats for **Fletcher**, **Harry** and **Rex**

    FLETCHER'S OFFICE
Desk. *On it*: desk lamp, phone, desk tidy, papers including newspaper cutting, notepad. *In drawer*: bottle of tranquillizers
Filing cabinet. *In drawer*: files, bottle of wine, glasses

Off stage: Pile of tabulations (**Rex**)
Shopping bag. *In it*: food shopping including large cream cake; brown paper bag containing glove puppet (**Osborne**)
Carrycot (**Ros**)

Personal: **Rex**: watch (worn throughout)
Fletcher: handkerchief, small comb
Ros: estimate
Osborne: pen, comb

SCENE 2

Re-set: Bottle of wine in cabinet

Off stage: Letters (**Norma**)

Personal: **Rex**: bottle of tranquillizers

SCENE 3

Off stage: Shopping (**Ros**)

LIGHTING PLOT

Practical fittings required: desk lamp
One interior with corridor backing and exterior backing beyond windows. The same
throughout

SCENE 1

To open: General interior "daylight" lighting on offices and corridor
with late morning effect on exterior backing

Cue 1   **Rex** gives a muffled sob   (Page 17)
Fade to black-out

SCENE 2

To open: General interior "daylight" lighting on offices and corridor
with early afternoon effect on exterior backing

Cue 2   **Rex** is left staring at the cutting   (Page 27)
Fade to black-out

SCENE 3

To open: General interior lighting from "overhead lights" on offices and corridor;
no light on exterior backing. **Fletcher**'s desk light on with covering spot

Cue 3   **Fletcher** switches off main lights   (Page 35)
Snap off main lights

Cue 4   **Fletcher** flicks off desk lamp   (Page 35)
Snap off covering spot

Cue 5   **Rex** switches on the lights   (Page 35)
Bring up main lights

Cue 6   **Rex** punches the air in victory   (Page 36)
Fade to black-out

CUT AND DRIED

CHARACTERS

Harry, mid-thirties
Rex, mid-thirties
Osborne, mid-twenties
Fletcher, mid-fifties
Norma, early twenties
Bryan Heath, forties
Ros, Rex's wife, mid-thirties

SYNOPSIS OF SCENES

The action of the play takes place in two adjoining offices in "Multiple Holdings"

Time — the present; six months after the action of *We Don't Want To Lose You*

CUT AND DRIED

SCENE 1

The offices of "Multiple Holdings". Six months after the action of "We Don't Want to Lose You". Late morning

Two offices are seen onstage. A corridor wall runs US *of the offices; the top section of this is made of reeded glass through which passers-by can dimly be seen. The larger office, to the* L, *is the general office; Fletcher's office is to the* R. *The offices are separated by a wood and glass partition with a door in it and a door leads out of the general office* US *into the corridor*

In the general office, facing DS, *are three desks, arranged in order of seniority, so the most senior desk, Rex's, is closest to Fletcher's office, Harry's desk is in the middle and that of Osborne, the most junior, is the furthest away. The desks have in and out trays and other office equipment on them and are piled high with ledgers and tabulations. Tall filing cabinets stand against the walls. There is a coatstand with coats on it for Fletcher, Harry, Osborne and Rex. Rex's umbrella is in evidence*

Fletcher's desk is spotlessly tidy, with a desk lamp, phone and papers on it. A deep swing chair and a filing cabinet are amongst the room's furnishings

When the CURTAIN *rises, Fletcher is reclining in the deep swing chair idly scanning a letter and sipping his coffee. There is a plate of biscuits on his desk. Rex is working alone in the general office*

Harry enters with a newspaper. He slowly and dramatically spreads the newspaper in front of Rex

Rex I haven't time for this, Harry.
Harry I think you might be interested …
Rex What is it?
Harry Here. In appointments. "International Company. Financial Accounting. Budgetary Control. Experience essential." No mention of qualifications. And it's in this area.
Rex (*interested*) Let me see.
Harry Look at the money …
Rex It's more than I get. I could do this job, Harry.

Harry You are doing.

Rex What!

Harry Read on. It's your job. The bastards have advertised your job — or rather Glover's job which you are now doing. How's that for a kick in the balls.

Rex But I understood it was to be an internal appointment.

Osborne enters

Osborne Glover's job's on the board. Apparently he's taking early retirement.

Rex I didn't know anything about this.

Osborne The doctor told him it was either retirement or death.

Harry It's in the *Telegraph* as well.

Osborne Let me see. (*He studies the paper*)

Harry Imagine seeing your own job advertised. Imagine how Rex feels.

Rex I was led to believe that the appointment would be made within the company.

Harry Well, what you're led to believe and what actually happens around here are two different things.

Rex I thought I'd be made permanent.

Harry According to this you've got a snowball's chance in hell of being made permanent.

Osborne They're obviously looking for a "whiz-kid"— a high flier.

Harry We don't want any "whiz-kids" around here showing us up. We're better off with someone like Rex.

Rex What?

Harry You'd better have a word with Fletcher.

Rex Don't worry, I'm going to …

Rex crosses to Fletcher's office, taps on the door, enters and closes the door carefully behind him. Harry and Osborne strain their ears to listen to the following

Rex May I have a word, JF?

Fletcher Well, I am rather busy. What is it?

Rex I wondered if you'd made any recommendations regarding my position here …

Fletcher Regarding your what?

Rex Position. I've been doing Glover's old job for several months now and ——

Fletcher I'm sorry, Rex. You've caught me on the hop here. Have we discussed this?

Rex More than once, JF. I was led to believe that my position would be ratified.

Fletcher Ratified?

Rex With regard to Glover's job. And that my salary would be back-dated and made substantive.

Fletcher Back-dated and made substantive. A tall order, Rex. Tell me, who told you this?

Rex You did. Now I find that Glover's job is being advertised.

Fletcher Yes — that was a surprise to me too. Sit down, Rex. Have a digestive.

Rex sits and chews solemnly on a biscuit

First of all, let me say you've done an excellent job. But we could have hardly ratified your position with poor Glover taking his first tottering steps towards recovery — the effect on him could have been catastrophic.

Rex But Glover's not coming back and the job's been advertised!

Fletcher Quite. And I want you to put in for it.

Rex Of course I'm going to put in for it! It's my job!

Fletcher With respect, Rex — that remains to be seen. We had to advertise the post — it's company policy. The Board insist that we cast our net as wide as possible — they feel there may be some big fish out there. I don't agree and I hope it'll be a mere formality.

Rex Hope! I've been doing this job for six months, on a low wage. I've balanced the accounts and brought them in on time — and you hope!

Fletcher I'll do my best, of course. (*He sighs*) Unfortunately you're not qualified …

Rex Neither are you.

Fletcher (*sharply*) We're not talking about me — we're talking about you.

Rex It didn't mention qualifications.

Fletcher No, and that's a good sign. They obviously didn't want to exclude you. On the other hand, that doesn't mean they don't value them. (*He dips his digestive in his coffee*) And then there's the question of age …

Rex Age?

Fletcher As we get older the brain cells begin to die, Rex. We become less supple, flexible, inventive. I've been aware of the process for some time. The brain is a muscle, Rex — use it or lose it. I just hope they're not looking for a younger man.

Rex A younger man! For years you've been saying I was too young for promotion — now you're saying I'm too old? When was I just right?

Fletcher I don't know, but we must have missed it. The trouble with age is it creeps up unnoticed, Rex. When I look in the mirror these days I see the face of a stranger.

Rex We're talking about me, JF.

Fletcher Well, now I look at you — you've certainly aged in the last few months. There are those little worry lines around your eyes.

Rex I'm not surprised!

Fletcher Rex, I say they may be looking for a younger man. I don't know. I'm not privy to their deliberations. I'll make my recommendation of course but the appointment is not within my gift. That's Bryan Heath's responsibility.

Rex Bryan Heath?

Fletcher PA to the MD. Known in the company as the Velvet Glove. What does that imply, Rex?

Rex An iron hand?

Fletcher Precisely. An iron hand capable of squeezing the juice out of a man and the pips as well. He'll be coming up to conduct the interviews — so make sure you're well prepared. The last man he interviewed for a post not only failed to secure the position — he lost the job he already had. Better start on your CV, Rex ...

Rex returns to the general office in a state of shock

Harry Well?

Rex He'll make his recommendations, of course ...

Harry Yes?

Rex He mentioned qualifications ...

Harry He's got a nerve. The only qualification he's got's a medal in ballroom dancing — and that's only a bronze.

Rex But he's not putting in for the job. He also mentioned age. He thought I may be too old.

Osborne and Harry study Rex

Harry You're not old.

Osborne It's just that you look old.

Rex That's what he said.

Harry It's not a beauty parade. You're doing the job — you should get it.

Rex Thanks, Harry.

Harry What worries me is if they do bring someone in from outside ... It could make one of us supernumarary.

Osborne Supernumerary?

Harry Think about it. We three have been doing this job for six months. They may think four's a crowd ...

Rex What are you talking about?

Harry I'm talking about redundancy.

Rex Not again. You're always talking about redundancy — it's all in your imagination. (*Pause*) You haven't heard anything, have you?

Harry Go to the washroom and leave your hands under the taps for a few minutes — you'll soon hear the whispers. Redundancy.

Rex But we're up to date. We've done a good job.

Harry Too good. They may feel they don't need us any more — well, not all of us …

Rex Don't talk like that in front of Osborne, Harry.

Harry Why not?

Rex It's not fair, because where redundancy is concerned the usual principle is: last in — first out.

Osborne What!

Harry Not necessarily — there's another principle. Highest paid — first out.

Rex Oh, yes, and there's another principle. Least missed — first out.

Harry There's no need to get personal. All I'm saying is, if one of us doesn't get Glover's job — we're in trouble.

Rex (*staring*) One of us?

Harry Well, I shall be putting in for it, that's obvious.

Rex Why? I'm doing the job, Harry. Unless they bring someone in from outside, surely it's a foregone conclusion.

Harry Of course it is. It's your job, Rex. But I have to show ambition.

Rex Do you?

Harry I'll be lucky to get an interview, I know that, but if I do, it'll be a good experience for me. It will also send a message to management …

Rex What message?

Harry That I'm not sitting back here perfectly content. It'll go on my record — this man has ambition.

Rex I could have told them that.

Osborne (*thoughtfully*) When's the closing date?

Rex stares at Osborne

Rex Not you as well?

Osborne I know I wouldn't get it. It's your job, Rex … But I have to remind Head Office that I exist.

Rex Do you think that's a good idea, Osborne? Don't you think it would be better if you kept it a secret?

Harry He won't even get an interview.

Osborne Why shouldn't I? At least I'm qualified.

Harry You should have been certified.

Rex You're too young, Osborne.

Osborne They maybe looking for someone younger. How would I feel if they gave the job to someone outside, even younger than I am and not so highly qualified?

Harry That's not likely to happen. As I've said, it's Rex's job.

Rex Right.

Harry But if there is a slip-up — I'd expect to be considered.

Rex Slip-up? What sort of slip-up?

Harry Well, say you have a terrible interview?

Rex Why should I have a terrible interview?

Harry Nerves. It can happen. You never know until you get in there. Some people forget their own names. All I'm saying is, that despite my unpopularity with management — I'd expect to be considered.

Rex What unpopularity?

Harry As you know I've always been too outspoken for my own good — I've made enemies. I know that. I've never been able to conform — always spoken my mind.

Rex What enemies? When have you spoken your mind? This is news to me.

Harry Whereas you've always been a born diplomat.

Rex A born diplomat? What do you mean?

Harry Smooth as silk.

Osborne (*darkly*) I hope it's going to be a fair contest.

Rex Wait a minute. A moment ago it was my job — now it's a contest. And what do you mean — fair?

Harry I think Osborne means you're well in with JF. That gives you an advantage.

Rex I'm not well in with JF.

Osborne You even finish his sentences for him.

Rex No, I don't.

Osborne At the end of the sentence, there you are, waiting.

Rex That's a lie.

Harry Rex, you'll get the job on merit — there's no need to dance attendance on him.

Rex When have you seen me dance attendance on him?

Osborne Yesterday, when you were coming in from the car park. You were sheltering him under your umbrella ...

Rex It was raining. What was I supposed to do?

Harry Let him get wet. I would have done. He can afford an umbrella.

Osborne I wouldn't have got wet for him.

Rex I wasn't getting wet. We were sharing it.

Harry Sharing an umbrella is a pretty intimate experience. You can do a lot of whispering under an umbrella.

Rex We weren't whispering.

Harry It demeans you, Rex. It looks sycophantic.

Osborne And what about the carrots?

Rex (*staring*) Wait a minute. How did carrots get into the conversation?

Harry At the annual dinner, in front of everyone, when you asked Fletcher if he'd care for your carrots.

Rex I don't like carrots.

Harry Well, I do, but I didn't notice any coming my way.

Osborne I wouldn't have given him my carrots, even if they were choking me.

Harry You see, to the casual observer, it looks ingratiating.

Rex Ingratiating! And what about your new interest in religion, Harry?

Harry (*uneasily*) What do you mean?

Rex I mean your Sunday morning visits to St Mary's. Quite a change from cleaning the car. It wouldn't be because Fletcher's a sidesman there?

Harry Certainly not.

Rex You were raised a Methodist, Harry — what are you doing in an Anglican church?

Harry It doesn't matter where you pray, Rex.

Rex That depends on what you're praying for — and who's listening. What are you praying for, Harry? Glover's job?

Harry Of course not. Just because we go to the same church doesn't mean we're close.

Rex You pray together: that's closer than sharing an umbrella.

Osborne (*thoughtfully*) I didn't know Fletcher went to St. Mary's.

Rex Forget it, Osborne — it's too late to get the ivory prayer book out now. Besides, Harry could be wasting his time. Fletcher can recommend but he's not making the appointment. Bryan Heath's coming down from head office.

Osborne Bryan Heath?

Rex Yes.

Osborne Then we're in trouble.

Rex Why?

Osborne He's trained in psychology. He analyses your character and looks for signs of inadequacy and mental instability. He appointed me.

Harry He can make mistakes then?

Osborne What do you mean? I did well in the tests. I've got a high IQ.

Harry Friend of mine took one of those psychological tests. They asked him to draw a snake — silly bugger drew a boa constrictor and failed.

Rex Why?

Harry Apparently the size of the snake indicates the size of your sexual drive. They thought he'd be nipping home each lunchtime for a bit of how's-your-father.

Rex I didn't know that.

Osborne What's your IQ, Rex?

Rex I've no idea.

Osborne You'd better find out. It's all IQ these days — especially if you're not qualified. I've got some tests in the drawer ... (*He searches through his desk drawer during the following*)

Harry I know a trick question. If a plane crashes on the border between France and Germany — and the passengers are Spanish — where do they bury the survivors?

Rex Wait a minute — let me think about this. France — Germany — Spanish ... Where do they bury the survivors? Harry, this isn't a trick question — it's a question of international law.

Osborne No, it isn't. You wouldn't bury the survivors.

Harry He certainly fell for that one.

Rex I wasn't thinking.

Osborne You were confused by detail. You should watch that. You have to see the clear picture.

Rex I know.

Osborne studies Rex thoughtfully

Osborne Tell me, Rex. When you see, say, a map of the Mediterranean in black and white — do you ever mistake the land for sea and the sea for land?

Rex Sometimes. Doesn't everyone?

Osborne Not people with high IQs.

Harry (*grinning*) I'd keep shovelling the carrots if I were you, Rex.

Fletcher enters the main office. He is grooming his moustache with a small comb. Rex stands up, smiling

Fletcher Well, I have to get off early, Rex. It's Monday again and — my …

Rex (*smiling*) Rotary lunch.

Fletcher Another boring …

Rex (*nodding*) Talk.

Fletcher Yes, by someone's who's been down the Amazon; wish the blighter had stayed there. (*He looks out of the window*) Hallo. Rain — I'll need ——

Rex Your mac, JF.

Rex takes Fletcher's mac from the coatstand and prepares to assist Fletcher on with it

Fletcher I wouldn't mind but the food's as boring as the talk. Always the same — boiled beef and …

Harry (*slyly*) Carrots?

Rex stops assisting Fletcher and abruptly hands him his coat. Fletcher looks mildly surprised. He crosses to the door and turns

Fletcher Oh, Harry, you were in fine voice on Sunday — you and Grace. I couldn't help noticing. I thought *He From Whom All Blessings Flow* was particularly fine. Keep that up and we'll have you in the choir.

Harry looks uncomfortable. Rex shoots him a withering glance. Fletcher checks the window again

Oh dear! Now it's pelting down. I shall get soaked.

Fletcher exits

Rex hesitates and then snatches up his umbrella

Rex Mr Fletcher …

Rex exits in pursuit

The Lights fade

CURTAIN

SCENE 2

The offices of "Multiple Holdings". Evening

When the CURTAIN *rises the Lights are burning in the general office. Rex is working alone at his desk*

Ros, Rex's wife, enters with a shopping bag

Rex Oh. Is that the time?
Ros I've been waiting ages. We were supposed to pick the children up from Mother's by seven.
Rex I've been busy.
Ros What are you doing?
Rex Tests. I need to concentrate. I couldn't do them at home. (*He sighs*) What am I talking about? I can't do them here!
Ros What tests?
Rex Ros — I've got an interview coming up and you ask what tests!
Ros There's no need to snap. You'll get the job, Rex — you're doing it.
Rex I still have to get through the interview.
Ros You will. Who else is there?
Rex There's always Harry.
Ros They wouldn't give it to Harry.
Rex Why not? Harry's very good at interviews. He makes an excellent first impression — a lousy second one, but that's not the point. And now he's warbling away in the choir at St Mary's — and Grace is trilling away with him. They're seeking divine intervention! And if Harry doesn't get it — there's always Osborne.
Ros You're joking.
Rex Apparently he has an extremely high IQ. He's some sort of prodigy. They say the line between genius and insanity is a fine one. I just hope he crosses it during the interview.

Ros Rex, stop worrying. I've learned one thing in life — no-one's as clever as we think.

Rex Good.

Ros On the other hand, no-one's as stupid either.

Rex That's what worries me. (*He throws down his pen*) What have I done with my life, Ros?

Ros You usually say that on your birthday. "What have I done with my life? Where am I going? And will I need false teeth?"

Rex They've stolen my life, Ros.

Ros Who have?

Rex The company. I've been here twenty years. I arrived young and full of hope, and look at me now.

Ros Cheer up, Rex. I've got a feeling that things are going to work out.

Rex (*with a bitter laugh*) Work out! You still think life's an equation, don't you? It's not an equation, it's a sum — a sum of days, months, years. And one day, when you're least expecting it, the great accountant in the sky draws the line, and that's it. "Rex Webber RIP".

Ros (*brightly*) Well, you've always wanted letters after your name.

Rex I'm glad you can still joke about it.

Ros You'll get there, Rex.

Rex Get there! I've had my bags packed for twenty years and I still haven't got there. I haven't even left the station. (*He sighs*) I wanted to be a success, Ros.

Ros You are a success.

Rex If I'm a success why am I wearing your father's suit? A suit I suspect he died in.

Ros He didn't. It was the blue one.

Rex I always wondered why your mother got upset when I wore the blue one.

Ros Rex, success isn't everything. Where did it get Mr Glover? Into Intensive Care.

Rex I know. And do you think I was sorry? No. I was willing it to happen — waiting for him to die.

Ros No — not deep down.

Rex Yes, deep down, I was willing it to happen. That's how it gets you. I was waiting for a dead man's shoes.

Ros Well, at least they'd go with the suit.

Rex I'm running out of time, Ros. The kids are growing up. One day they'll want wine with their meals and to go to college, and I won't be able to provide those things — and do you know why? Because I'm a failure.

Ros You're not a failure — and you will get that job.

Rex I hate interviews. My shirt starts to prickle and my mind goes blank. I respond to the questions like a sheep with brain damage.

Ros You mustn't feel like that. You're a handsome, intelligent man. When you walk into a room, all heads turn.

Rex Which way?

Ros They note the bright eyes, the humorous mouth. You can depend on this man; you feel easy with him. This man could deal with any situation, adapt to change, be calm in a crisis. The room lights up with warmth and good fellowship. This is the man we're looking for.

Rex stares at her in awe

Rex Do you see me like that?

Ros *(after a pause)* Well, no, not exactly; but if you don't value yourself, Rex — no-one else will.

Rex Ros, we're only talking about the interview — and my shirt's started to prickle.

Ros But surely Mr Fletcher's recommendation will be the deciding factor.

Rex It might. But which way is he going to jump. These Anglicans stick together.

Ros Harry isn't Anglican — he's Methodist.

Rex Ros — Harry would turn Muslim to get Glover's job.

Ros That's underhand.

Rex I know.

Ros *(after a pause)* Rex, why don't we invite Mr and Mrs Fletcher round for dinner?

Rex What!

Ros If they're doing it — why shouldn't we?

Rex Because it would be creeping. And suppose they found out? My name would be mud. Dinner … They even objected to a few carrots!

Ros I don't see how they can object. Harry and Grace are meeting him in church.

Rex Church is different — at least it's in front of witnesses. God's there for one thing. But inviting him to the house — even Harry wouldn't stoop to that. It's fawning. I can just see it.

Rex bows in a fawning manner

"Welcome to my humble abode, Mr Fletcher. Excuse the frayed carpet and the children's finger-marks — and mind the roller-skates. And if you'd care to use me as a doormat the pleasure will be entirely mine." I don't need to stoop that low.

Ros Are you sure? You don't seem to be doing very well with those tests. What are you trying to do?

Rex Find my IQ.

Ros Haven't you got one?

Rex Of course I've got one. Everyone's got one — even you.

Ros What do you mean — even me?

Rex Well, it's just that yours won't be high. It's not your fault. But the brain's
like a muscle — if you don't use it, you lose it. And yours has been dulled
by domestic routine.

Ros Has it really? And how high is your IQ?

Rex I don't know. I'm trying to find out by doing these puzzles.

Ros Puzzles. You mean like the ones we do with the children?

Rex Well, more sophisticated than that — but that sort of thing.

Ros Oh dear.

Rex What do you mean — "Oh dear"?

Ros You're not very good at those.

Rex What makes you say that?

Ros You couldn't find your way through the maze to feed Trixie's rabbits
last night.

Rex This is a little more complicated than finding a way through to feed
Trixie's rabbits, Ros.

Ros And you couldn't find the six little gnomes hiding in the garden.

Rex For God's sake! I'm not interested in six little gnomes hiding in the
garden! We're talking applied logic here.

Ros Let me see. (*She picks up the paper and reads*) "Underline the odd one
out. Dorf, Revor, Teylenb. And Doncroc."(*She gives a puzzled frown*)

Rex (*smiling*) You see — you're not with it, are you? They're anagrams.

Ros I can see they're anagrams. That's Ford, Rover, Bentley … Ah, it's
Doncroc, isn't it?

Rex (*staring*) Doncroc?

Ros That's Concord, it's an aeroplane — the others are cars.

Rex (*after a pause*) Yes, well, that's obvious, isn't it? Trust you to pick an
easy one.

Ros Here's another odd one out. "House — igloo — bungalow — office."

Rex I've done that one. It's igloo.

Ros Why?

Rex It's the only one made of ice.

Ros No.

Rex What do you mean — no?

Ros It's office. You live in a house, igloo and bungalow. You don't live in
an office. They threw igloo in to confuse you.

Rex (*after a hesitation*) I suppose that is an alternative answer..

Ros (*reading on*) "Find the missing numbers. 7, 10, 9, 12, 11: what are the
next two?

Rex I've been puzzling over that. You see, they start to get difficult.

Ros (*promptly*) 13 and 14.

Rex What?

Ros 13 and 14.

Rex Anyone can say that, Ros. Anyone can say 13 and 14.

Ros There are two series here. Each rising by two. So it's 13 and 14.

Rex What an incredible fluke.
Ros No — I find them easy. (*She continues to study the tests*)

Rex watches Ros

Rex They've done this on Woman's Hour, haven't they?
Ros No. (*She becomes engrossed*)
Rex Ros, if a plane crashed on the German/French border, and the passengers
    were Spanish — where would they bury the survivors?
Ros They wouldn't bury the survivors, Rex, there'd be complaints.

Rex throws his pen down in despair

    What's the matter?
Rex I've just discovered something. I have an IQ lower than the average
    housewife. Well, do you know what a man does in this world when he has
    no qualifications and a low IQ?
Ros No, what does he do?
Rex He invites the boss round for dinner.

The Lights fade

CURTAIN

SCENE 3

The offices of "Multiple Holdings". Late morning

When the CURTAIN *rises, Rex, Harry and Osborne are at their desks. Rex is
wearing a smart blue suit, cut a little generously*

Rex moves to the filing cabinet. Harry studies him

Rex What's the matter?
Harry You look different this morning. Is that a new suit?
Rex Yes. (*He tugs awkwardly at his jacket*)
Harry Is it yours?
Rex (*defiantly*) It was made to measure,
Harry Who for?

Osborne sniggers

Rex What are you sniggering at, Osborne?
Osborne It smells of mothballs.
Harry You seem to be making a special effort these days, sartorially
    speaking ... Is it because of the job?
Rex The interviews aren't until Thursday, Harry.

Harry No, but Heath's coming down today, isn't he?

Rex Is he? I wondered why you were wearing the cufflinks.

Harry What?

Rex I couldn't help noticing. You've been shooting your cuffs all morning. Gold cufflinks. Be careful, Harry — they'll think you don't need the money.

Osborne My mother puts all her faith in clean underwear.

Rex That won't do you much good, unless you're planning a striptease.

Harry He'd do more than that to get Glover's job.

Osborne I won't get Glover's job. I'm just happy to have made the shortlist.

Rex I bet you are.

Harry It won't matter what we wear. They've made their minds up about us years ago. (*Darkly*) It's all in the file … (*He nods towards Fletcher's office*)

Osborne What file?

Harry The personnel file he keeps in the locked drawer of his desk. The one he refers to during the annual salary review. Highly confidential — it contains our character assessments.

Osborne Is there a highly confidential file, Rex?

Rex If Harry hasn't seen it, it must be.

Norma enters. She smiles warmly at Rex and moves to the filing cabinets

Harry Of course there's a file — it's in a black cover. It has all our little weaknesses written down. Isn't that right, Norma?

Norma How would I know?

Harry You're his secretary.

Norma And that's why I'm not discussing it.

Harry But you're not denying it, are you? What does it say about me, Norma?

Norma I haven't read it.

Harry But there's a file, isn't there? (*Broodingly*) What's in it? There's something, some black mark, something I did, or said, years ago — still being held against me …

Rex Well, there can't be anything good about me. I've been stuck here for years. They must have something against me.

Osborne Not necessarily. They say that everyone rises according to his ability until he reaches a position that's beyond his powers — and there he remains — completely useless.

Rex Congratulations — you've arrived, Osborne.

Harry If I knew there was something in that file about me — something detrimental — I'd sue him for slander.

Rex No, if he calls you incompetent and lazy, that's slander. If he writes it down, that's libel.

Norma Not if it's true.
Harry (*indignantly*) Who says it's true?
Rex Norma's right. It could be fair comment — a matter of opinion. But if
he were to write down that you were a sneaky, underhand schemer — that
would be libel.
Norma Not if it's true.

Harry frowns

Norma exits

Rex Besides, it's confidential — not to be read by others, in which case your
reputation has not been damaged.
Harry Of course it's read by others. Bryan Heath for example. It won't be
confidential from him. The only people it's confidential from are us!

Fletcher enters from the corridor. He sniffs

Fletcher Is there a smell of mothballs in here? (*He goes into his office,
unlocks a drawer and takes a black file from it. He studies the file*)

*Rex hesitates for a moment and then hitches up his trousers and sidles in after
Fletcher. Harry watches Rex suspiciously. As Rex enters, Fletcher slides the
black file he's been studying back into the drawer and locks it*

Fletcher Yes, Rex?

*Rex closes the door behind him carefully and approaches very close to
Fletcher*

Rex (*in a low voice*) JF — my wife and I wondered if you and Mrs Fletcher
were free this evening ...
Fletcher (*staring*) What was that?
Rex (*almost whispering*) If you were free this evening — we wondered if
you'd care to come to dinner ...
Fletcher (*astonished*) Dinner? At your house?
Rex Sh!
Fletcher What?

Rex casts an anxious glance towards the general office

Rex I know it's short notice — and I'd quite understand if you're busy. It's
just that we just have this leg of pork that isn't doing anything ...
Fletcher This evening ...

Rex You've got something on — I quite understand. Perhaps another time..
Fletcher Rex, I would be delighted to come to your house..
Rex (*surprised*) Would you?
Fletcher But unfortunately, this evening …
Rex Out of the question — I thought so.
Fletcher There's Bryan Heath, you see.
Rex Of course.
Fletcher He's staying at the Royal. He'll expect me to join him for, er …
Rex Dinner. I understand. Perhaps another time, JF.
Fletcher I'll look forward to it.
Rex So will I.

Rex looks relieved. He edges out of the office. He returns to his desk

Harry Why did you close the door?
Rex I always close the door.
Osborne I think the less time anyone spends in that office with the door closed the better.
Rex He was looking at that file, Harry.
Harry The file in the black cover?
Rex Yes.
Harry What did I tell you? He's going to reveal all our little failings to Bryan Heath. We have a right to know what's in that file.
Rex He keeps the key on his key ring.
Harry There's always a spare …
Rex Well, I don't know where it is.
Harry No, but Norma does.
Rex She won't tell.
Harry She'll tell you.
Rex Why?
Harry Because she fancies you. God knows why but she does. Ask her.
Rex I can't do that. It would be a breach of trust. She could lose her job.
Harry Rex, you've got to look out for yourself in this life. If you've got an angle, use it. You've got this edge with Norma, we haven't. If we can find out what's in that file we'd be prepared. Now, if you can get close to Norma … What do you say, Osborne?
Osborne He smells of mothballs.
Harry So what! She's not a bloody moth.

Fletcher enters from his office. He clears his throat importantly

Fletcher Would you put your pens down — those who are actually using them — and listen. I've just had a call from reception. (*Dramatically*) Bryan Heath has entered the building. We have been invited by the manager to take drinks with him in the boardroom. Bryan Heath is a shrewd man with a penetrating stare that can turn you to jelly. So let caution be your watchword. Don't drink too much. *In vino veritas*. Do you know what that means, Osborne?

Osborne Out of the wine comes truth.

Fletcher It had better not. He may ask you questions about matters here. Answer him in a frank and honest manner but don't tell him anything. Where Head Office is concerned we're as one. Now come with me ...

Fletcher exits. Harry and Osborne follow

Rex pauses to straighten his suit

Norma returns with more papers

Norma Aren't you going up?

Rex In a moment.

Norma That's right. Always arrive late.

Rex Why?

Norma That way you'll be noticed. And when you get there, stand in the middle of the room — that's where all the important people stand. Corners are for nobodies.

Rex (*smiling*) I'll remember that. You want me to get this job, don't you?

Norma Yes.

Rex Why?

Norma You know why. Not that it means anything.

Rex But it does. (*He moves closer to Norma*) Norma, I want the spare key to Fletcher's drawer.

Norma I can't do that!

Rex If I can see that file, it may give me an advantage.

Norma It may get me the sack.

Rex No-one would know. I'd put it back. All I need is a quick glance. You do want me to get the job ... (*He pulls her gently to him*)

Norma (*sniffing*) Mothballs.

Rex But you're not a moth.

Norma No, but I must have the brains of one listening to this. You haven't taken much notice of me lately. Why now?

Rex Norma, I've noticed you but it wouldn't have been fair. What could I have done for you on my salary? You'd have become bored with me. I couldn't afford an affair.

Norma (*surprised*) An affair?

Rex You need to be in senior management for that. And suppose Ros found out? I certainly couldn't afford a divorce.

Norma Divorce!

Rex It could happen. Does that surprise you?

Norma Divorce — yes … I'm still getting used to the affair.

Rex And it needn't end with Glover's job. Fletcher won't last much longer. He has the look of a man who's heard the call of the sea. And if I were to get Fletcher's job … it could mean trips away … if you get my meaning.

Norma pulls away and stares at Rex for a moment

Norma The spare key's in amongst the paper clips. We haven't talked about this — and I don't know anything about it …

Norma exits

Rex winces and looks ashamed of himself for a moment. He crosses to Fletcher's office, finds the key and removes the black file from the drawer. He returns to his desk and opens the file

Bryan Heath appears, standing in the doorway. He is a man in his forties with strong features, broad shoulders. He is wearing a smart city overcoat. He watches Rex

Rex realizes he is being watched

Heath Excuse me. I seem to have lost my way. I was looking for the boardroom.

Rex It's on the next floor. I'll take you. It's Mr Heath, isn't it?

Heath Yes. You must be Rex Webber.

Rex (*smiling*) How did you know?

Rex closes the file as Heath advances

Heath Desk piled high with work — head down — always the last to leave. You answer the description. Is that JF's office?

Rex Yes.

Heath Quite a contrast. One might think you're really running this show …

Rex I wouldn't say that.

Heath No, perhaps you're right. Appearances can be deceptive. A man with a crowded desk and his head down often misses what's going on around him. He doesn't see the bigger picture. Do you know what I mean?

Rex I think so.

Heath He gets bogged down in detail — and he misses opportunities … Opportunities for advancement … (*Pause*) I like your report on the bad debt situation, by the way, it was very informative.

Rex (*pleased*) I did spend some time on it.

Heath And it showed. Perhaps we could talk about it further, that and the general situation here — and the problems you've been experiencing. What about dinner this evening?

Rex This evening?

Heath I'm on my own — nothing to do.

Rex Well, I'm not sure that …

Heath Bring your wife — unless you feel she may be bored.

Rex No — she'd be fascinated. She's absolutely dedicated to the company, but …

Heath Then what's the problem?

Rex I think JF may have arranged something for you.

Heath (*with a conspiratorial smile*) JF? No, I don't think so. I mean, JF's all right …

Rex Yes …

Heath I like him …

Rex So do I …

Heath But …

Rex I know …

Heath A little bit …

Rex Boring?

Heath Yes — a bit of an old …

Rex Woman?

Heath Should we say eight o'clock?

Rex At the Royal?

Heath No, I'll find somewhere more interesting. Perhaps I could pick you up.

Rex At the house?

Heath Well, yes.

Rex Actually, I have some work to finish. Perhaps you could pick us up here?

Heath Certainly. Eight o'clock then.

Fletcher enters. He regards Rex and Heath suspiciously

Fletcher Ah, there you are, Bryan. They're waiting for you.

Heath Just coming.

Fletcher Sorry I wasn't here to greet you. Did you want me to book a table for this evening?

Heath Ah, sorry — no.

Fletcher (*surprised*) No?

Heath Prior engagement. Next floor, isn't it?

Heath exits followed by Fletcher

Rex is about to follow then remembers the file. He picks it up

  Harry and Osborne enter and regard Rex suspiciously

Harry Where have you been?
Rex I was delayed.
Osborne You were talking to Bryan Heath.
Harry Were you trying to impress him by working to the last minute?
Rex No.
Harry You were up to something. (*He sees the file in Rex's hand*) You've
  got the file! (*He snatches it from Rex*)
Rex I was putting it back. I haven't looked at it. On reflection I don't this is
  ethical.
Harry (*flicking through the file*) Bugger ethical. This isn't ethical. This is the
  Star Chamber. Trial without jury — without the accused being present. (*He
  stops suddenly and looks shocked*)
Rex What is it?
Harry My God!
Rex What is it?
Harry Listen to this. (*He reads*) "There is no doubt about his ambition but
  the form it takes is not particularly attractive. He is inclined to be
  ingratiating and all things to all men. He wants to be liked and leaves
  unpopular decisions to others. He may not have the necessary qualities for
  leadership ..." (*He strikes the desk with the file*) How's that for character
  assassination?
Rex I'm sorry, Harry. I know you've got your faults, we all have. But I don't
  see you like that.
Harry That's not me, that's you.
Rex What!
Harry (*reading on*) No, he calls me a schemer who enjoys office politics and
  stirring up trouble. Me!

Rex and Osborne exchange glances

Osborne What does it say about me?

  Harry checks the file

Harry Apparently you're a dreamer and out of touch with reality.
Osborne (*shocked*) A dreamer! (*He slumps down at his desk*)

Rex takes the file from Harry and studies it

Rex (*bitterly*) So this is what's held me back all these years. "Ingratiating" — "all things to all men". I could sue him.
Harry I wouldn't. (*He pats Rex's shoulder*) I mean, there are elements …
Rex Elements?
Harry That one might recognize …
Rex (*indignantly*) What elements? Ingratiating! Wants to be popular! All things to all men!
Harry They're the ones.
Rex You mean, you see me like this? What do you think, Osborne?
Osborne Don't ask me, Rex. I'm a dreamer.

Fletcher appears in the corridor; his shadowy presence is visible

Harry (*seeing Fletcher*) Someone's coming!

Fletcher comes into the office. Rex slips the file into his drawer

Fletcher Ah, Rex. Bryan Heath is asking for you. Apparently you've made quite an impression. And what are you doing, Osborne? You're supposed to be helping with the refreshments.
Osborne (*coldly*) Sorry, Mr Fletcher, I must have been *dreaming…*

Osborne, Rex and Harry stare at Fletcher with hostility; Fletcher becomes aware of this

Fletcher Oh, Rex, since Bryan Heath has a prior engagement it does mean I'll be able to accept your kind invitation.

Silence. Osborne and Harry look at Rex

Rex Invitation?
Fletcher For dinner.
Rex Sorry. It's off.
Fletcher Off?
Rex Ros rang. Bad news from the nursery. Mumps.
Fletcher Mumps! (*He moves back*) Oh, I believe they can be dangerous to a man of mature years.
Rex Very.
Fletcher Pity … (*He moves to the door*)
Harry (*softly*) All things to all men..
Fletcher (*turning*) Should we make it tonight then, Harry?
Harry What?

Fletcher You were going to give me a hand erecting the greenhouse.

Rex's and Osborne's hostility turns on Harry. He becomes aware of this

Harry Sod your greenhouse!

    Harry barges out

The Lights fade

CURTAIN

SCENE 4

The offices of "Multiple Holdings". Evening

When the CURTAIN *rises, the office is deserted except for Rex. He is wearing his top coat and pacing up and down*

Ros bursts in wearing an evening coat and looking flustered

Ros Am I late?
Rex No, he is. Did you get your hair done?
Ros My God! Can't you tell?
Rex You look flustered.
Ros Of course I'm flustered. I couldn't get a sitter. I had to take them over to Mother's. She wasn't pleased. She said she hoped it was important.
Rex Of course it's important. This evening could affect my whole career.
Ros I don't know why you couldn't have come home first.
Rex Because he'd have called and seen the gate off its hinges, the peeling paintwork, and the ten year-old Sierra rusting in the drive! He'd have judged me by that. Besides, I wasn't leaving here — not until they'd gone. I didn't want them getting Heath to themselves.
Ros Why not?
Rex Because they'd have bad-mouthed me.
Ros How do you know?
Rex Because that's what I'd do to them.
Ros (*shocked*) You wouldn't.
Rex Wouldn't I? That's what I intend to do tonight. First opportunity, in with the poison — no more the diplomatic silence. If he wants to know about those two — my God, I'll tell him.
Ros Rex, you can't. You're not like that.
Rex Aren't I? How do you know what I'm like? There are some very different views on that.

Ros What are you talking about?

Rex If I were to describe someone to you as ingratiating, eager to please, all things to all men, someone in the company — and I'm not talking about Harry. Who would you say it was? (*He stops*) Why are you smiling?

Ros It's you, isn't it?

Rex (*aghast*) You recognize me from that?

Ros Not exactly. There is another way of looking at it. You want to be loved, you're kind, and you don't like hurting people.

Rex Well, it's time I changed. I won't get Glover's job that way.

Ros At least you can sleep at nights.

Rex I don't want to sleep at nights. I want to lie there hating myself. I've had twenty years with a clear conscience, and where's it got me?

Ros But you can't change just like that.

Rex Can't I? You'd be surprised. (*Pause*) I already hate myself.

Ros You mean because of tonight?

Rex Not just tonight. That's the least of my worries.

Ros Suppose the others find out?

Rex What if they do?

Ros Won't it look like creeping?

Rex I'm not creeping — I'm climbing. And you've got to help me.

Ros How?

Rex Why do you think Heath invited you? Because wives are important. I've known men fail in the company because their wives weren't acceptable. He'll be expecting to meet a corporate wife. He'll want to get a good look at you. Did you get the dress?

Ros Yes, but it was such a rush — you'll probably hate it.

Rex Let me see.

Ros takes her coat off to reveal an attractive, if a little low cut, dress. Rex regards her in silence for a moment

Rex Well, he's certainly going to get a good look at you in that.

Ros Is there something wrong?

Rex No. Can you keep it up?

Ros Of course I can keep it up. You think it's too low?

Rex No. (*He smiles*) Just watch out for the jelly and ice cream.

Ros You hate it.

Rex No. (*Pause*) As a matter of fact, it brought back a memory. You had a dress like that years ago. And when you walked into a room with me I'd swell with pride.

Ros (*staring*) You were proud of me?

Rex Yes.

Ros You never said.

Rex Didn't I? (*He moves and looks out of the window*)

Ros And now it's just a memory? I mean, you don't any more?

Rex What?

Ros Feel proud of me?

Rex I want to feel proud of you tonight. That's a nice perfume. Come here.

Ros (*moving closer*) Not too strong?

Rex No, at least it'll hide the smell of these mothballs. I don't know why your father was so addicted to them — it was the camphor that probably killed him.

Ros Rex!

Rex Heath will probably take us to a French restaurant — so don't order anything you can't pronounce. And don't talk about the children all the time. He's looking for a poised, sophisticated woman and you lack confidence.

Ros (*drily*) I wonder why.

Rex It's not your fault — it's because you're at home all the time. Whereas Grace is a woman of the world.

Ros Grace? How did Grace come into this?

Rex She's bound to enter the equation. If Harry's got an edge he'll use it. He'll find a way of introducing her to Heath.

Ros (*coldly*) What do you mean — edge?

Rex Grace was privately educated, she's travelled, she speaks several languages — she has this veneer.

Ros (*sharply*) If she has, it cracked a long time ago.

Rex She also has this way of speaking — without moving her lips.

Ros (*staring*) Why should she do that?

Rex I suppose it's so you can't look into her mouth..

Ros Probably frightened you'll see the forked tongue.

Rex No — they all do it.

Ros Who do?

Rex Well-bred people.

Heath enters and stands by the door

Ros Well-bred! She's boring. And I don't care how many languages she can speak — she'll be boring in every one of them. She could bore for England. And why does she walk around with her arms folded with that cardy draped over her shoulders — like a teacher on playground duty?

Rex I don't know.

Ros Do you think it's because she hasn't a bust?

Rex Of course she has a bust.

Ros She hasn't. When the company took us to Spain last year — she went topless for three days and no-one even noticed.

Rex I didn't know about that.

Ros Of course not — it was a non-event.

Rex I don't know why you're getting so irritated. I was merely pointing out her attributes.

Ros Well, she can take her attributes and stuff them where the sun doesn't shine!

Heath, at the door, claps his hands, amused. Rex and Ros turn and see him

Heath I can see it's going to be an interesting evening.

Rex (*in an affected voice*) Oh. We didn't see you. Sorry about that.

Ros registers the change in Rex's voice

Heath Please, don't apologize. You didn't tell me your wife was so spirited, Rex.

Rex Oh, yes, Bryan — this is Rosalind.

Ros looks surprised

Heath Rosalind — I haven't heard that name for a long time.

Ros (*drily*) Neither have I.

Heath I've booked a table at the *Café Bleu*. Is that all right?

Rex Oh, yes. It's frightfully good, isn't it, Rosalind?

Ros (*raising her eyebrows*) Frightfully.

They move towards the door

Fletcher enters. He gapes in surprise

Heath   Working late, John?

Fletcher I was passing. I saw the lights.

Heath   Well, we're just leaving. We'll leave you to switch them off.

Heath, Rex and Ros exit

Fletcher stares after them

Fletcher (*grimly*) Mumps…! The bastard.

The Lights fade

CURTAIN

The offices of "Multiple Holdings". A few days later. Evening

When the CURTAIN *rises, the office is in darkness. There are lights on in the corridor. There are distant sounds of conversation and laughter*

The door from the corridor opens and Osborne enters, switching the lights on. He holds a glass in his hand. He is wearing a smart suit but his tie is awry. He slumps down at his desk.

Rex enters a moment later. He is also holding a glass. He regards Osborne anxiously

Rex Are you all right, Osborne?

Osborne (*who clearly isn't all right*) Fine. I just don't know why he can't get it over with. Why can't he call us? It's been three days since the interview.

Rex Perhaps he hasn't made up his mind.

Osborne He's made up his mind. That's why we're having this reception.

Rex Osborne, he's going back to Head Office, the reception is to say goodbye and thank you ——

Osborne Don't you believe it. We all know who's got the job. He's just dragging it out. He's a sadist. I can't eat a thing.

Rex That's because you're drinking too much.

Osborne It was always cut and dried. And what really pisses me off is that I had a terrific interview.

Rex Did you?

Osborne I didn't put a foot wrong. But I suppose he held my youth against me.

Rex We don't know that.

Osborne Don't you? (*Pause*) He asked me if I was married. I'm always getting asked that. They seem to prefer married men. I said I was getting engaged but I don't suppose it made any difference.

Rex (*surprised*) Getting engaged! I didn't know about this. Who's the lucky girl?

Osborne I don't know. I haven't met her yet. (*Pause*) I suppose you think I shouldn't have said that?

Rex No — never let the truth get in the way of a good interview, Osborne.

Osborne I told him I believed in marriage — that it was for life and that I didn't believe in casual affairs.

Rex Osborne — he's divorced.

Osborne Shit!

Rex He lives with his secretary.

Osborne How do you know?

Rex He told me.

Osborne Oh, yes — I was forgetting. You've been socializing with him.

Rex Ros and I had dinner with him — that's all.

Osborne No — that's not all.

Rex It was the only time.

Osborne That's not what I heard ...

Rex What do you mean?

Osborne I've also heard that this little reception is in your honour.

Rex You sure? Where did you hear this?

Osborne I heard Fletcher telling the manager. I always knew it was cut and dried.

Rex Osborne, it's the first I've heard of it. And it was never cut and dried. I would point out he asked Harry and Grace out to dinner as well.

Osborne He never asked me out to dinner.

Rex Well, look on the bright side — he may have asked you to bring your fiancée.

Osborne You can laugh. (*Mysteriously*) I just hope this doesn't blow up in your face, Rex.

Rex What are you getting at?

Osborne I think you know what I'm getting at. (*He rises*) Undue influence ...

Osborne staggers out

Rex sits at his desk. The frown passes from his face and finally he leans back in his chair and begins to smile

Norma enters. She looks towards the corridor

Norma Is he all right?

Rex Too much to drink, that's all. (*He leans further back in his chair*)

Norma What are you doing here?

Rex Enjoying the moment. I've been sitting in this chair for months, not knowing if it was going to be mine. Now I've just heard something that makes me feel it will be.

Norma Good. (*She leans forward to kiss Rex*)

Rex Not now. I can't risk that — not at the moment.

Norma Are you frightened Bryan might find out?

Rex Norma, no-one under the rank of Senior Assistant calls him Bryan.

Norma I think I can call him Bryan. I feel I can call any man by his first name once he's tried to get inside my pants.

Rex (*shocked*) He tried that?

Norma He's known for it. That's why his wife left him.

Rex Oh. Still, we have to be careful.

Norma Why? You've got the job.

Rex How do you know?

Norma Ask Ros.

Rex How would she know?

Norma Perhaps he told her over drinks ...

Rex What drinks?

Norma He asked me to have drinks with him at the Royal one lunchtime.
I refused. Then I changed my mind — I suppose it was curiosity. He was
with Ros in the cocktail bar. They were in animated conversation.

Rex Ros? I don't believe it.

Norma She's having an affair with him. That's why you've got the job.

Rex Not Ros — I know her.

Norma Do you? She's a bored housewife, Rex. At home all day wondering
whether to have a nervous breakdown or make a casserole. Pacing around
the house, the level in the sherry decanter getting lower and lower, so
frustrated she's ready to hurl herself through the double glazing ... And then
Bryan Heath comes along ...

Rex No, not Ros. You don't know her.

Ros enters

Norma kisses Rex gently on the cheek

Norma Don't looked so shocked, Rex. After all, you don't really mind, do
you? Not so long as you get the job ... (*She straightens up and sees Ros by
the door, watching them*)

Norma brushes by Ros and exits

Ros and Rex regard each other in silence for a moment

Ros What were you two doing?

Rex (*sharply*) What were we doing? What were you doing?

Ros What?

Rex In the cocktail bar of the Royal with Bryan Heath.

Ros (*after a pause*) Who told you?

Rex Norma. Apparently he sent out several invitations — you just happened
to be first in line. What happened?

Ros We talked.

Rex I know about the talk. It was animated. What did you talk about?

Ros Him mostly. He said he was shy, and quite a lonely person — lacking
in confidence since his wife left him.

Rex Did you believe that?

Ros No.
Rex Then what happened?
Ros Nothing.
Rex Nothing! They why didn't you tell me?
Ros I couldn't.
Rex And I know why you couldn't. You had drinks in a bar with Bryan Heath
and talked about loneliness. What did you think was going to happen? Why
did you go?
Ros I thought I was helping. Isn't that what you wanted?
Rex Not that sort of help. It didn't end with talking about loneliness, did it?
Ros No. He asked me to go up to his room. I refused.
Rex Then why have I got the job?
Ros Have you?
Rex Yes, thanks to you.

Ros moves to the door

Where are you going?
Ros I'm not going back in there. I'll wait for you in the car.
Rex You mean you can't face them?
Ros I mean I can't take any more of Grace's trilling laugh every time Bryan
Heath says something. It's giving me a headache. You should have married
Grace. She's the corporate wife. Sophisticated, well-bred, all that education.
She can say yes in any language …
Rex (*staring*) What?

Ros exits

Rex looks down at Glover's chair. Suddenly, in a fury, he kicks it over

Harry enters. He stares at Rex and picks the chair up

Harry They're waiting for you in the boardroom. Where's Ros?
Rex In the car. She's got a headache. (*He moves to the door*)

Harry detains Rex

Harry While we're on our own, old mate. Something I want to say. Bryan
said it would be all right. I told him we'd been friends for a long time —
that it would be better coming from me. I've got Glover's job.
Rex (*sitting*) What?
Harry I had a great interview — apparently I was head and shoulders above
the rest. (*He pats Rex's shoulder*) But don't be too depressed. You won't
have long to wait — and then the job's yours.

Rex How do you know?

Harry Because I have it on good authority that JF is past his sell-by date. And I shall be moving into there. And after that Head Office.

Rex Head Office! Did Bryan Heath tell you all that?

Harry (*after a hesitation*) Not exactly. It was something he told Grace. Strictly confidential. He said they needed fresh blood at headquarters.

Rex He told Grace that?

Harry Well, she's been showing him around and they got talking. They get on very well — similar backgrounds. They have this rapport.

Rex They must have.

Harry Well, he knows Grace is the soul of discretion. She can keep a secret.

Rex She told you.

Harry Yes, but we're man and wife.

Rex (*smiling*) Yes, I was forgetting.

Harry I must say, Rex, I'm relieved. I thought you'd be bitter. I didn't think you'd take it with a smile.

Rex Neither did I. Still, the race isn't always to the swiftest, Harry.

Harry That's the spirit. (*He looks around*) Now, I'm supposed to be looking for JF's glasses. He's supposed to make a speech. (*He enters Fletcher's office; during the following he sits in Fletcher's chair*)

Rex takes his coat from the stand

   Fletcher enters

Fletcher Rex, they're waiting for you.

Rex They can wait. I'm going.

Fletcher Ah. So Harry's told you?

Rex Yes.

Fletcher It simply wasn't within my gift. I hope you understand.

Rex Yes … What I don't understand is why they want me up there, if I haven't got the job?

Fletcher It's a little surprise. You may not be aware of this but it's twenty years to this very day since you joined the company, a fresh-faced schoolboy. Bryan Heath is to present you with a long service certificate and an eight day clock.

Rex A clock!

Fletcher Suitably inscribed — and with Westminster chimes. A proud moment, Rex.

Rex Is it? Well, you can tell Heath to stick his clock.

Fletcher I can't tell him that! Obviously the disappointment has been too much for you.

Rex On the contrary, I'm not disappointed and I'm taking my wife out to celebrate.

Fletcher But you haven't got the job.
Rex I know but according to Harry I won't have long to wait..
Fletcher What do you mean?

Rex nods towards Fletcher's office and exits

*Fletcher stares into his office. Harry, sitting in Fletcher's chair, swings
gently to and fro. Their eyes meet*

The Lights fade

CURTAIN

FURNITURE AND PROPERTY LIST

On stage: GENERAL OFFICE
Tall filing cabinets containing files
Three desks. *On them*: in and out trays, ledgers, tabulations, office
  equipment, etc.
Chairs
By **Rex**'s *desk*: **Rex**'s umbrella
Coatstand. *On it*: coats for **Fletcher**, **Harry**, **Osborne** and **Rex**

FLETCHER'S OFFICE
Desk. *On it*: desk lamp, phone, desk tidy with key in it, papers, letter,
  plate of biscuits, cup of coffee. *In drawer*: black file
Deep swing chair
Filing cabinet. *In drawer*: files

Off stage: Newspaper (**Rex**)

Personal: **Fletcher**: small comb

SCENE 2

Set: IQ tests on **Rex**'s desk

Off stage: Shopping bag (**Ros**)

Personal: **Fletcher**: desk key

SCENE 3

No additional props

SCENE 4

No additional props

SCENE 5

Off stage: **Osborne**: glass
Rex: glass

LIGHTING PLOT

Practical fittings required: desk lamp
One interior with corridor backing and exterior backing beyond windows. The same throughout

SCENE 1

To open: General interior "daylight" lighting on offices and corridor
with late morning effect on exterior backing

Cue 1   **Rex**: "Mr Fletcher …". He exits in pursuit   (Page 51)
Fade to black-out

SCENE 2

To open: General interior lighting from "overhead lights" on offices and corridor;
no light on exterior backing

Cue 2   **Rex**: "He invites the boss round for dinner."   (Page 55)
Fade to black-out

SCENE 3

To open: General interior "daylight" lighting on offices and corridor
with late morning effect on exterior backing

Cue 3   **Harry**: "Sod your greenhouse!" He barges out   (Page 64)
Fade to black-out

SCENE 4

To open: General interior lighting from "overhead lights" on offices and corridor;
no light on exterior backing

Cue 4   **Fletcher**: "Mumps …! The bastard."   (Page 67)
Fade to black-out

SCENE 5

To open:	Interior lighting from "overhead lights" on corridor only; no light in offices or on exterior backing	
Cue 5	**Osborne** switches the lights on *Snap on "overhead lights" in office*	(Page 68)
Cue 6	**Fletcher**'s and **Harry**'s eyes meet *Fade to black-out*	(Page 73)

EFFECTS PLOT

Cue 1   As SCENE 5 begins   (Page 68)
                Distant sounds of conversation and laughter;
                  fade under dialogue